The
BATHROOM
FOOTBALL
ALMANAC

———— • ————

by

Jeff Kreismer

RED-LETTER PRESS, INC.
Saddle River, New Jersey

THE BATHROOM FOOTBALL ALMANAC
COPYRIGHT ©2017 Red-Letter Press, Inc.
ISBN-13: 9781603871563
ISBN: 160387156X

All Rights Reserved
Printed in the United States of America

Red-Letter Press, Inc.
P.O. Box 393
Saddle River, NJ 07458

www.Red-LetterPress.com

ACKNOWLEDGMENTS

EDITORIAL:
Jack Kreismer

•

BOOK DESIGN & TYPOGRAPHY:
Jeff Kreismer

•

COVER ART:
Design by Damonza

•

RESEARCH & DEVELOPMENT:

Kobus Reyneke
Mike Ryan
Jim Tomlinson

The
BATHROOM
FOOTBALL
ALMANAC

JANUARY

On This Date: On January 1, 2015, four teams took part in the first-ever College Football Playoff in two semi-final contests. Oregon beat Florida State in the Rose Bowl, while Ohio State topped Alabama in the Sugar Bowl. Ohio State would later beat Oregon for the National Championship, 42-20.

Birthdays: Doak Walker, 1927; Frank Minnifield, 1960; Derrick Thomas, 1967; Stephen Tulloch, 1985; Jason Pierre-Paul, 1989; Darius Slay, 1991

Trivia: Which two college football teams vie for the Little Brown Jug?

Trivia Answer: Michigan and Minnesota

JANUARY

On This Date: On January 2, 1965, Joe Namath signed his first contract with the New York Jets for the then-unheard of sum of $400,000. The charismatic quarterback from little Beaver Falls, PA, quickly adjusted to life in the Big Apple - especially the nightlife - earning the nickname "Broadway Joe."

Birthdays: Gino Marchetti, 1927; Pat Fischer, 1940; Al Denson, 1942; Calvin Hill, 1947; Raymond Clayborn, 1955; Craig James, 1961; Scott Mitchell, 1968; Ronald Darby, 1994

Trivia: Joe Namath elected to sign with the AFL's Jets after what NFL team also drafted him?

Trivia Answer: St. Louis Cardinals

JANUARY

On This Date: On January 3, 1993, the Buffalo Bills overcame a 32-point deficit, the largest in NFL history, to win 41-38 in overtime and eliminate the Houston Oilers from the playoffs.

Birthdays: Hank Stram, 1923; David Little, 1959; Jim Everett, 1963; Charles Johnson, 1972; David Tyree, 1980; Eli Manning, 1981; DeShone Kizer, 1996

Trivia: In 1980, what team pulled off the biggest regular season comeback in NFL history after trailing the Saints, 35-7, at halftime?

Trivia Answer: San Francisco 49ers, who won 38-35

JANUARY

On This Date: On January 4, 2006, Vince Young scored on a last-second touchdown run to give his Texas Longhorns a thrilling 41-38 win over USC in the Rose Bowl and claim the national title. Young was named the MVP with 267 yards passing, 200 yards rushing and three touchdowns. Texas' come-from-behind victory snapped a 34-game Trojans win streak.

Birthdays: Johnny Lujack, 1925; Don Shula, 1930; Kermit Alexander, 1941; George Atkinson, 1947; Jackie Harris, 1968; Garrison Hearst, 1971; Todd Sauerbrun, 1973; Michael Griffin, 1985; Eric Weddle, 1985; Steve Slaton, 1986

Trivia: What squad did Vince Young dub the "Dream Team" after signing with them in 2011?

Trivia Answer: Philadelphia Eagles

JANUARY

On This Date: On January 5, 2003, the 49ers defeated the Giants in a Wild Card postseason game, 39-38, in historic fashion. The Giants blew a 38-14 lead as San Francisco scored 25 unanswered points in the second half. New York botched a 41-yard field goal attempt as time expired that would have won it.

Birthdays: Chuck Noll, 1932; E.J. Holub, 1938; Jim Otto, 1938; Sam Wyche, 1945; Mercury Morris, 1947; Warrick Dunn, 1975; Corey Chavous, 1976; Eric Fisher, 1991; Phillip Dorsett, 1993

Trivia: What team blew a 28-point lead in their 45-44 loss to the Colts in the 2013 postseason?

Trivia Answer: Kansas City Chiefs

JANUARY

On This Date: On January 6, 2002, Michael Strahan fell on Brett Favre to break the NFL's single-season sack record with 22.5. The future Hall of Famer would finish his career with 141.5 QB takedowns.

Birthdays: Lou Holtz, 1937; Harold Jackson, 1946; Howie Long, 1960; Sean Landeta, 1962; Charles Haley, 1964; Tim McDonald, 1965; Keenan McCardell, 1970; James Farrior, 1975; Asante Samuel, 1981; A.J. Hawk, 1984; Ndamukong Suh, 1987; Jameis Winston, 1994

Trivia: What 2009 football film includes footage from Lawrence Taylor's 1985 sack of Joe Theismann, which caused Theismann's career-ending leg injury?

Trivia Answer: The Blind Side

JANUARY

On This Date: On January 7, 2008, #2-ranked LSU took down #1 Ohio State, 38-24, in the BCS National Championship Game in New Orleans. Matt Flynn threw four TD passes as his team became the first two-loss squad to win a national title.

Birthdays: Eddie LeBaron, 1930; Brian Baldinger, 1959; Ron Rivera, 1962; Bobby Engram, 1973; Scott Wells, 1981; Michael Sam, 1990

Trivia: What two LSU stars who entered the league in 2014 share the NFL record for the most receptions in a player's first three seasons, with 288?

Trivia Answer: Odell Beckham Jr. and Jarvis Landry

JANUARY

On This Date: On January 8, 2000, the Music City Miracle took place when the Titans beat the Bills in the playoffs. A Frank Wycheck lateral allowed Kevin Dyson to score the game-winning touchdown off the kickoff after Buffalo had just taken the lead with seconds left. Exactly 12 years later, the Broncos experienced their own playoff miracle when Tim Tebow hit Demaryius Thomas for an 80-yard score to beat the Steelers in overtime.

Birthdays: Dwight Clark, 1957; Darryl Williams, 1970; Billy Joe Hobert, 1971; Blair Walsh, 1990; Isaiah Crowell, 1993

Trivia: In 1975, a new football term was coined when the Cowboys beat the Vikings in a playoff game on a last-second 50-yard touchdown pass. On the miracle score, Roger Staubach said, "I closed my eyes and said a Hail Mary." Who caught it?

Trivia Answer: Drew Pearson

JANUARY

On This Date: On January 9, 2000, Dan Marino recorded the final victory of his NFL career when his Dolphins beat the Seahawks, 20-17, in the playoffs. The contest would be the final game ever played at Seattle's Kingdome. Marino's squad would advance to face Jacksonville, where they would be demolished 62-7 the following week.

Birthdays: Bart Starr, 1934; Dick Enberg, 1935; Chad Johnson, 1978; John Henderson, 1979; Justin Blackmon, 1990; Marcus Peters, 1993

Trivia: Dan Marino teamed up with what comic actor in the 1994 film *Ace Ventura: Pet Detective?*

Trivia Answer: Jim Carrey

JANUARY

On This Date: On January 10, 1982, the Cincinnati Bengals iced the AFC championship with a 27-7 win over the San Diego Chargers. More notable than the score were the temperature (nine below zero) and the wind chill (59 below), making this "Freezer Bowl" the coldest playoff game on record.

Birthdays: Steve Jordan, 1961; Hollis Thomas, 1974; Jake Delhomme, 1975; Clark Haggans, 1977; DeShaun Foster, 1980; Landon Collins, 1994

Trivia: In 1988, the Bears defeated the Eagles in a Divisional Playoff contest that became known by what name because of the extreme weather conditions at Soldier Field?

Trivia Answer: The Fog Bowl

JANUARY

On This Date: On January 11, 1987, John Elway led his Broncos on "The Drive", marching 98 yards for a touchdown and ultimately beating the Cleveland Browns in the AFC Championship Game. Elway's heroics only tied the game, as Denver would need an overtime field goal to prevail, 23-20.

Birthdays: Freddie Solomon, 1953; Richmond Webb, 1967; David DeCastro, 1990; Malik Jackson, 1990

Trivia: The season after "The Drive", what Brown was responsible for "The Fumble" near Denver's goal line with Cleveland about to tie the score late in the 1987 AFC Championship?

Trivia Answer: Earnest Byner (The Browns lost, 38-33.)

JANUARY

On This Date: On January 12, 1969, the Jets' $400,000 investment in Joe Namath matured. The New Yorkers - almost three touchdown underdogs - made good on their outspoken quarterback's guarantee of victory and shocked the Baltimore Colts, 16-7, in Super Bowl III.

Birthdays: Tom Dempsey, 1947; Drew Pearson, 1951; Henry Thomas, 1965; Cade McNown, 1977; Chad Greenway, 1983; Justin Houston, 1989

Trivia: "After (Super Bowl III), we could have played the Girl Scouts and we wouldn't have taken it as a joke." What Colts tight end said it?

Trivia Answer: John Mackey

JANUARY

On This Date: On January 13, 1974, the Miami Dolphins, behind 145 yards rushing from MVP Larry Csonka, defeated the Minnesota Vikings, 24-7, in Super Bowl VIII. Miami, appearing in their third consecutive Super Bowl, became the second team (after Green Bay) to win back-to-back titles.

Birthdays: Kent Hull, 1961; Curtis Conway, 1971; Bam Morris, 1972; Nick Mangold, 1984; Josh Freeman, 1988; Morgan Burnett, 1989; Doug Martin, 1989

Trivia: Bart Starr was the first player to win back-to-back Super Bowl MVP awards. Who was the second?

Trivia Answer: Terry Bradshaw

JANUARY

On This Date: On January 14, 1973, the Miami Dolphins defeated the Washington Redskins, 14-7, to win Super Bowl VII. In doing so, they became the first NFL team to go undefeated over an entire season.

Birthdays: Fred Arbanas, 1939; Gene Washington, 1947; Carl Weathers, 1948; Kyle Brady, 1972; Byron Leftwich, 1980; Vincent Jackson, 1983; Brandon Meriweather, 1984; Jon Beason, 1985; Hakeem Nicks, 1988

Trivia: What two quarterbacks led the Miami Dolphins to their perfect 1972 season?

Trivia Answer: Bob Griese and Earl Morrall

JANUARY

15

On This Date: On January 15, 1967, the Green Bay Packers beat the Kansas City Chiefs, 35-10, in the first game between champions of the NFL and AFL - or Super Bowl I. Bart Starr earned MVP honors.

Birthdays: Randy White, 1953; Kenny Easley, 1959; Drew Brees, 1979; Brandon Mebane, 1985; Glover Quin, 1986; Luke Willson, 1990

Trivia: While the Packers-Chiefs meeting is now referred to as "Super Bowl I", what name was the event originally given?

Trivia Answer: The First AFL-NFL World Championship Game

JANUARY

16

On This Date: On January 16, 1972, the Dallas Cowboys earned their first Super Bowl victory with a 24-3 win over the Miami Dolphins. In the loss, the Dolphins became the only team not to score a touchdown in the history of the game.

Birthdays: Dave Brown, 1953; Jim Caldwell, 1955; Kevin Ross, 1962; Joe Horn, 1972; Mario Bates, 1973; Joe Flacco, 1985; Jonathan Allen, 1995

Trivia: In 2016, what team won their first postseason contest in over 20 years by recording the first shutout win in an NFL playoff game in a decade?

Trivia Answer: Kansas City Chiefs, who beat the Texans 30-0

JANUARY

On This Date: On January 17, 1999, the heavily favored Vikings fell to the Atlanta Falcons in the NFC Championship Game in overtime, 30-27. Minnesota's Gary Anderson, who did not miss a single kick the entire regular season, failed to convert a 38-yard attempt that could have sealed it in regulation for his team.

Birthdays: Buddy Dial, 1937; Preston Pearson, 1945; Dick Ambrose, 1953; Ted Thompson, 1953; Derrick Mason, 1974; Dominic Rhodes, 1979; Koa Misi, 1987

Trivia: What Viking missed a chip-shot 27-yard field goal attempt with seconds remaining that would have given Minnesota the lead over Seattle in the 2015 playoffs?

Trivia Answer: Blair Walsh

JANUARY

On This Date: On January 18, 2015, the Patriots advanced to Super Bowl XLIX after routing the Colts, 45-7. While the blowout was impressive, the game will most be remembered as the origin of the "Deflategate" scandal.

Birthdays: Tobin Rote, 1928; Julius Peppers, 1980; Chris Snee, 1982; Latavius Murray, 1990; Leonard Fournette, 1995

Trivia: What Patriots owner claimed that Russian President Vladimir Putin "stole" his Super Bowl ring in 2005?

Trivia Answer: Robert Kraft

JANUARY 19

On This Date: On January 19, 2002, the Patriots snuck past the Raiders, 16-13, in a snowy Divisional Playoff Game. New England was aided by a call in which a Tom Brady fumble was changed to an incomplete pass as a result of the now infamous "Tuck Rule." A few clutch kicks by Adam Vinatieri enabled New England to escape in overtime.

Birthdays: Joe Schmidt, 1932; Dan Reeves, 1944; Steve DeBerg, 1954; Ottis Anderson, 1957; Junior Seau, 1969; Tyrone Wheatley, 1972; Walter Jones, 1974; Elvis Dumervil, 1984

Trivia: In which Patriots Super Bowl victory did Adam Vinatieri *not* make the game-winning kick: XXXVI (Rams), XXXVIII (Panthers) or XXXIX (Eagles)?

Trivia Answer: XXXIX (Eagles)

JANUARY 20

On This Date: On January 20, 1991 and 2008, the New York Giants advanced to the Super Bowl with game-winning field goals. Matt Bahr accounted for all of New York's scoring in a 15-13 win over the 49ers in the 1990 NFC title game. Exactly 17 years later, it was Lawrence Tynes connecting to defeat Green Bay, 23-20, in overtime.

Birthdays: Milt Plum, 1935; Bill Kenney, 1955; Mark Stepnoski, 1967; Eddie Kennison, 1973; Rae Carruth, 1974; Jeremiah Trotter, 1977; Cullen Jenkins, 1981; Rey Maualuga, 1987; Nick Foles, 1989; DeVante Parker, 1993

Trivia: What former kicker for the New York Giants was John Madden's longtime broadcast partner?

Trivia Answer: Pat Summerall

JANUARY

On This Date: On January 21, 1979, Terry Bradshaw threw four touchdown passes as his Steelers got by the Cowboys, 35-31, to win Super Bowl XIII. With the win, Pittsburgh became the first team in NFL history to win three Super Bowls.

Birthdays: Gary Garrison, 1944; Billy "White Shoes" Johnson, 1952; Jacob Green, 1957; Dalton Hilliard, 1964; David Harris, 1984; Haloti Ngata, 1984; Peyton Hillis, 1986

Trivia: What Olympic figure skater was once married to Terry Bradshaw?

Trivia Answer: Jo Jo Starbuck

JANUARY

On This Date: On January 22, 1984, Raiders running back Marcus Allen ran for a then-Super Bowl record 191 yards as L.A. took Super Bowl XVIII with a 38-9 victory over the Redskins. Exactly five years later, in Super Bowl XXIII, Jerry Rice set a record that still stands with 215 yards receiving in a 20-16 49ers win over the Bengals.

Birthdays: Lou Creekmur, 1927; Joe Perry, 1927; George Seifert, 1940; Lester Hayes, 1955; Jason Peters, 1982; Ray Rice, 1987; Ty Montgomery, 1993

Trivia: What Hall of Famer holds the record for the most career yards rushing in the Super Bowl?

Trivia Answer: Franco Harris, with 354

JANUARY

On This Date: On January 23, 1983, the Dolphins defeated the Jets, 14-0, in the AFC Championship Game. The contest became known as the "Mud Bowl" due to its less-than-desirable playing conditions. New York had complained about Miami's decision not to place a tarp over the wet, muddy Orange Bowl field before the game.

Birthdays: Jerry Kramer, 1936; Pat Haden, 1953; Frank Winters, 1964; Eric Metcalf, 1968; Kevin Mawae, 1971; Phil Dawson, 1975; Lavonte David, 1990

Trivia: What team was denied five Super Bowl trips when they lost all but one of their AFC Championship Games in the 1970s?

Trivia Answer: Oakland Raiders

JANUARY

On This Date: On January 24, 1982, the San Francisco 49ers beat the Cincinnati Bengals, 26-21, in Super Bowl XVI. The 49ers held on to a 20-0 halftime lead, and despite being out-gained in total yardage 356 to 275, won their first ever Super Bowl championship.

Birthdays: Bobby Bryant, 1944; Bill Bradley, 1947; Chris Warren, 1968; Tim Biakabutuka, 1974; Brian Cushing, 1987

Trivia: In Super Bowl XVI, what Bengals receiver caught 11 passes for two touchdowns?

Trivia Answer: Dan Ross

JANUARY

25

On This Date: On January 25, 1987, the New York Giants defeated the Denver Broncos, 39-20, to win their first Super Bowl. Game MVP Phil Simms set a record by going 22 of 25 passing. He threw for 304 yards and three touchdowns.

Birthdays: Lou "The Toe" Groza, 1924; Don Maynard, 1935; Mark Duper, 1959; Mark Schlereth, 1966; Brent Celek, 1985; Patrick Willis, 1985; Danny Woodhead, 1985

Trivia: After Super Bowl XXI, Phil Simms became the first Super Bowl MVP to utter what now-famous phrase on TV?

Trivia Answer: "I'm going to Disney World!"

JANUARY

26

On This Date: On January 26, 1986 and 1997, the New England Patriots lost in their first two Super Bowl appearances. In Super Bowl XX, the Pats were destroyed, 46-10, by the Chicago Bears. In '97, they were defeated by the Packers, 35-21, in Super Bowl XXXI.

Birthdays: Henry Jordan, 1935; Jack Youngblood, 1950; Merril Hoge, 1965; Eric Davis, 1968; Dan Bailey, 1988; Torrey Smith, 1989; Manti Te'o, 1991

Trivia: What Colts Hall of Famer coached the New England Patriots to their first Super Bowl appearance in 1986?

Trivia Answer: Raymond Berry

JANUARY

On This Date: On January 27, 1991, Scott Norwood's "wide right" 47-yard field goal attempt enabled the Giants to hold on for a 20-19 win over the Bills in Super Bowl XXV.

Birthdays: Fritz Pollard, 1894; Art Rooney, 1901; Cris Collinsworth, 1959; Matt Stover, 1968; Bryant Young, 1972; Fred Taylor, 1976; Stevan Ridley, 1989

Trivia: Whose missed 32-yard field goal would have tied the Ravens with the Patriots in the closing seconds of the 2011 AFC Championship Game?

Trivia Answer: Billy Cundiff

JANUARY

On This Date: On January 28, 2001, the Baltimore Ravens won their first NFL championship, blowing out the New York Giants, 34-7, in Super Bowl XXXV. The history-making 2000 Ravens defense allowed just 10.3 points per game during the regular season. That average dropped to under six per game in their four postseason wins.

Birthdays: Charlie Krueger, 1937; Jon Jansen, 1976; Daunte Culpepper, 1977; Stephen Gostkowski, 1984

Trivia: After the Ravens first Super Bowl win, "Goose" said of the team's White House visit, "I'm a little depressed they didn't have a buffet." Who is he?

Trivia Answer: Tony Siragusa

JANUARY

On This Date: On January 29, 1995, Steve Young set a Super Bowl record with six passing touchdowns as his 49ers took down the San Diego Chargers, 49-26, in Super Bowl XXIX.

Birthdays: Bill Nelsen, 1941; Tony Galbreath, 1954; Andre Reed, 1964; Aeneas Williams, 1968; Rob Bironas, 1978

Trivia: A matchup of what two teams in 2015 resulted in a stunning 52-49 final score and an NFL record of 13 combined touchdown passes?

Trivia Answer: The Saints defeated the Giants as Drew Brees threw seven TD passes and Eli Manning six.

JANUARY

On This Date: On January 30, 1983, the Redskins defeated the Dolphins in Super Bowl XVII. Because Washington owner Jack Kent Cooke had already won the NBA crown in 1972 with the Lakers, he became the first person to own title-winning franchises in two major sports.

Birthdays: Nolan Cromwell, 1955; Chris Slade, 1971; Deltha O'Neal, 1977; Cameron Wake, 1982; Bashaud Breeland, 1992

Trivia: What Kansas City owner coined the phrase "Super Bowl"?

Trivia Answer: Lamar Hunt

JANUARY

On This Date: On January 31, 1988, the
Redskins dominated the Broncos, 42-10, in Super
Bowl XXII. Exactly five years later, the Cowboys destroyed
the Bills, 52-17, in SB XXVII. Quarterbacks Doug Williams and
Troy Aikman earned respective MVP honors.

Birthdays: Don Hutson, 1913; Earl Faison, 1939;
Louis Wright, 1953; Doug Pederson, 1968; Michael Sinclair, 1968;
Vernon Davis, 1984; Mario Williams, 1985

Trivia: What two Super Bowl-winning quarterbacks share the
NFL record for touchdowns without an interception in an entire
postseason, with 11?

Trivia Answer: Joe Flacco and Joe Montana

FEBRUARY

On This Date: On February 1, 2015, the Patriots
won Super Bowl XLIX, 28-24, after one of the game's most
unbelievable finishes. Rookie Malcolm Butler intercepted
Seattle's Russell Wilson on New England's one-yard line with
seconds left. Exactly 11 years earlier, the Pats won Super Bowl
XXXVIII over the Panthers in another thriller, 32-29. Tom Brady
claimed both MVPs.

Birthdays: Clark Gaines, 1954; Wade Wilson, 1959;
Rob Ninkovich, 1984

Trivia: Are the Patriots the only NFL team to ever win three
titles in a four-year span?

Trivia Answer: No - The Cowboys did it first in the 1990s.

FEBRUARY

On This Date: On February 2, 2014, the Seattle Seahawks embarrassed the Denver Broncos, 43-8, in Super Bowl XLVIII. Denver's record-setting regular season offense did not get on the board until the end of the third quarter. The Super Bowl was the first to be held outdoors in a cold-weather environment, at New Jersey's MetLife Stadium.

Birthdays: George Halas, 1895; Wayne Fontes, 1940; Dexter Manley, 1958; Mike Tice, 1959; Ken Dilger, 1971; Donald Driver, 1975; Cortland Finnegan, 1984; Kawann Short, 1989; Harrison Smith, 1989

Trivia: The Cowboys beat the Broncos in the first-ever indoor Super Bowl (XII), played in a city that has hosted double-digit Super Bowls. What's the venue?

Trivia Answer: New Orleans Superdome

FEBRUARY

On This Date: On February 3, 2008, the New York Giants shocked the football world and the undefeated Patriots, beating New England, 17-14, in Super Bowl XLII. Six years earlier to the day, the Pats pulled off their own stunner when they won their first title with a 20-17 win over the Rams in Super Bowl XXXVI.

Birthdays: Fran Tarkenton, 1940; Bob Griese, 1945; John Jefferson, 1956; Dennis Smith, 1959; Jeff Christy, 1969; Kris Dielman, 1981; Julio Jones, 1989; James White, 1992

Trivia: With just four catches during the regular season, what Giant made the miracle helmet grab that led to New York's Super Bowl XLII upset over the Patriots?

Trivia Answer: David Tyree

FEBRUARY

On This Date: On February 4, 2007, the Colts defeated the Bears, 29-17, to win Super Bowl XLI. Peyton Manning won his first ring (and MVP honors), as rain fell for the first time throughout an entire Super Bowl.

Birthdays: Harry Jacobs, 1937; Lawrence Taylor, 1959; Jerome Brown, 1965

Trivia: Which player has not caught a Super Bowl touchdown pass from Peyton Manning: Marvin Harrison, Reggie Wayne or Pierre Garçon?

Trivia Answer: Harrison

FEBRUARY

On This Date: On February 5, 2017, the Patriots stunned the Atlanta Falcons in Super Bowl LI, 34-28. The Pats overcame a 28-3 deficit, the largest in the game's history, and prevailed in the first Super Bowl overtime on a two-yard James White TD run. Tom Brady claimed a record fourth MVP.

Birthdays: Roger Staubach, 1942; Craig Morton, 1943; Rich Saul, 1948; Charle Young, 1951; Dirk Koetter, 1959; Laurence Maroney, 1985; Kelvin Benjamin, 1991

Trivia: Who is the only quarterback to be named Super Bowl MVP without throwing a touchdown in the game?

Trivia Answer: Joe Namath (Super Bowl III)

FEBRUARY

On This Date: On February 6, 2011, the Packers defeated the Steelers, 31-25, in Super Bowl XLV. Over 100,000 were on hand at Cowboys Stadium to see Green Bay claim their fourth Super Bowl victory. Aaron Rodgers, with 304 yards passing and three touchdowns, was named MVP.

Birthdays: John Dutton, 1951; Carl Lee, 1961; Tom Tupa, 1966; Jermaine Kearse, 1990

Trivia: In Super Bowl XLV, what Packer, who had 582 yards receiving on the season, set career highs in the game with nine receptions for 140 yards?

Trivia Answer: Jordy Nelson

FEBRUARY

On This Date: On February 7, 2016, the Broncos shut down the Panthers to win Super Bowl 50, 24-10. The event would be the final game in the career of Peyton Manning. Exactly six years earlier, Manning suffered his first Super Bowl defeat (XLIV) as the Colts fell to the Saints, 31-17.

Birthdays: Jeff Van Note, 1946; Robert Brazile, 1953; Rolf Benirschke, 1955; Tim Bowens, 1973; Matthew Stafford, 1988; Morris Claiborne, 1990; Markus Wheaton, 1991

Trivia: True or False? Peyton Manning is the only starting quarterback in Super Bowl history to win the game with two different teams.

Trivia Answer: True

FEBRUARY

On This Date: On February 8, 1936, in an effort to offset the dominance of the Giants and Bears, the NFL conducted the first college draft. The Eagles used the first pick to select University of Chicago running back Jay Berwanger.

Birthdays: John Fox, 1955; Raleigh & Reggie McKenzie, 1955; Terry McDaniel, 1965; Marcus Pollard, 1972; Johnny Hekker, 1990

Trivia: What nickname is given to the very last pick of the NFL Draft every year?

Trivia Answer: Mr. Irrelevant

FEBRUARY

On This Date: On February 9, 2002, the AFC defeated the NFC, 38-30, in the Pro Bowl. In the victory, Rich Gannon became the first player to claim back-to-back Pro Bowl MVP honors since the NFL began naming just one MVP in 1973.

Birthdays: Bill Bergey, 1945; Danny White, 1952; Mike Kenn, 1956; Jimmy Smith, 1969; Logan Ryan, 1991

Trivia: What QB was the MVP of the 1978 Rose Bowl, the 1997 Pro Bowl, and is a member of the Canadian and Pro Football Halls of Fame?

Trivia Answer: Warren Moon

FEBRUARY

On This Date: On February 10, 1997, a jury ordered O.J. Simpson to pay $25 million in punitive damages to the families of Nicole Brown Simpson and Ronald Goldman. That judgment was on top of $8.5 million in compensatory damages awarded the previous week when Simpson was found liable for their deaths in a civil trial.

Birthdays: Cornell Green, 1940; Dick Anderson, 1946; Daryl Johnston, 1966; Wayne Gandy, 1971; Ty Law, 1974; C.J. Anderson, 1991

Trivia: True or False? O.J. Simpson is the only player to rush for 1,000 yards in a single season in both the AFL and NFL.

Trivia Answer: False - It's Mike Garrett.

FEBRUARY

On This Date: On February 11, 1997, Bill Parcells was introduced as the new head coach of the New York Jets. The NFL legend would transform the one-win Jets into a winner in a single season and reach the AFC title game the year after that.

Birthdays: Gary Barbaro, 1954; Daryn Colledge, 1982; Barry Church, 1988; Jake Matthews, 1992

Trivia: Bill Parcells has been the head coach of how many NFL teams?

Trivia Answer: Four (Giants, Patriots, Jets and Cowboys)

FEBRUARY

On This Date: On February 12, 1937, Cleveland was granted an NFL franchise. The team, still in existence today, would play in Ohio until 1946, when they moved to Los Angeles to become the Rams.

Birthdays: Mark Bortz, 1961; Brent Jones, 1963; Lincoln Kennedy, 1971; DeMarco Murray, 1988; Robert Griffin III, 1990; Paxton Lynch, 1994

Trivia: In December of 1995, the Browns played their last NFL game in Cleveland before moving to Baltimore for the following season. The event also marked the final game ever played at what venue?

Trivia Answer: Municipal Stadium (The Browns beat the Bengals, 26-10.)

FEBRUARY

On This Date: On February 13, 1937, owner George Marshall moved the Boston Redskins to Washington, D.C., where they promptly won an NFL championship in their first year, defeating the Chicago Bears, 28-21.

Birthdays: Eddie Robinson, 1919; Ruben Brown, 1972; Charlie Garner, 1972; Randy Moss, 1977; Mike Brown, 1978; Drew Henson, 1980; Michael Turner, 1982; Aqib Talib, 1986; Charles Clay, 1989

Trivia: When it comes to pageantry, the Redskins were the first NFL team to have one of these. What?

Trivia Answer: An official marching band

FEBRUARY 14

On This Date: On February 14, 1966, CBS purchased the rights to the 1966 and 1967 NFL Championship Games for $2 million per game. Today's Super Bowl television advertising rates have surpassed $5 million for a 30-second spot alone.

Birthdays: Woody Hayes, 1913; Jim Kelly, 1960; Jeff Graham, 1969; Drew Bledsoe, 1972; Steve McNair, 1973; David Garrard, 1978; Alshon Jeffery, 1990; Jadeveon Clowney, 1993; Christian Hackenberg, 1995

Trivia: CBS televised Super Bowl I along with what other network?

Trivia Answer: NBC

FEBRUARY 15

On This Date: On February 15, 2014, Ravens running back Ray Rice and his fiancée Janay Palmer were arrested for simple assault over an incident that took place in an Atlantic City casino. Once details emerged, Rice would be suspended by the NFL and released by Baltimore before the start of the season.

Birthdays: Abe Woodson, 1934; Gene Hickerson, 1935; John Hadl, 1940; Ken Anderson, 1949; Darrell Green, 1960; Edgar Bennett, 1969; Kenny Vaccaro, 1991

Trivia: Ray Rice recorded the second-longest postseason run in NFL history with an 83-yard TD on the first play from scrimmage in Baltimore's 2009 playoff game against what team?

Trivia Answer: New England Patriots

FEBRUARY 16

On This Date: On February 16, 1959, Tim Mara, the founder of the New York Giants, died at the age of 71. The Hall of Famer, who paid $500 for the franchise, built the Giants into a perennial contender during his tenure with the team.

Birthdays: Jerome Bettis, 1972; Ahman Green, 1977; Todd McClure, 1977; Kyle Fuller, 1992

Trivia: What Baltimore Colts receiver went on to become the founder and majority owner of the Carolina Panthers over three decades later?

Trivia Answer: Jerry Richardson

FEBRUARY 17

On This Date: On February 17, 1936, Jim Brown was born. Arguably the best running back in NFL history, Brown spent nine record-setting years with the Cleveland Browns from 1957-65.

Birthdays: Buddy Ryan, 1934; Jim Brown, 1936; Dennis Green, 1949; Stanley Morgan, 1955; Neil Lomax, 1959; Guy McIntyre, 1961; Bryan Cox, 1968; Levon Kirkland, 1969; Case Keenum, 1988; Taylor Gabriel, 1991

Trivia: In addition to being honored by both college and pro football, what other sports Hall of Fame is Jim Brown a member of?

Trivia Answer: Lacrosse

FEBRUARY

On This Date: On February 18, 2002, the
Houston Texans held their expansion draft, choosing
19 players in all. Pro Bowl tackle Tony Boselli of the
Jaguars was the first selection.

Birthdays: George Gipp, 1895; Len Ford, 1926;
Bob St. Clair, 1931; Brian Waters, 1977; Brandon Flowers, 1986;
Le'Veon Bell, 1992

Trivia: At 19, the youngest player ever drafted by an NFL team
was the 10th overall pick in 2007 by the Texans. Who is he?

Trivia Answer: Amobi Okoye

FEBRUARY

On This Date: On February 19, 2011, Hall of
Fame running back Ollie Matson died at the age of 80.
When Matson retired in 1966, his 12,799 career all-purpose
yards were second only to Jim Brown.

Birthdays: Paul Krause, 1942; Roger Goodell, 1959;
William Henderson, 1971; Dwight Freeney, 1980

Trivia: The first running back in NFL history to have
1,000-yard seasons for three different teams did so with the
49ers, Eagles and Seahawks. Who is he?

Trivia Answer: Ricky Watters

FEBRUARY

On This Date: On February 20, 1967, Buffalo Bills quarterback Jack Kemp accepted a "permanent off-season job" on California governor Ronald Reagan's staff. It was the beginning of Kemp's political career, as he was the Republican candidate for the Vice Presidency in the election of 1996.

Birthdays: Roy Zimmerman, 1918; Gill Byrd, 1961; Fred Jackson, 1981

Trivia: What U.S. President was credited with introducing the forward pass to American football in 1906?

Trivia Answer: Theodore Roosevelt

FEBRUARY

On This Date: On February 21, 1968, the National Football League agreed to recognize the NFL Players Association as the exclusive bargaining agent for its athletes.

Birthdays: Ernie McMillan, 1938; Terry Allen, 1968; Braylon Edwards, 1983

Trivia: What Colts Hall of Famer became the first President of the NFL Players Association in 1970?

Trivia Answer: John Mackey

FEBRUARY

On This Date: On February 22, 1967, the "sling-shot" goal post was made standard in the NFL. However, the actual field goal posts themselves would not be moved to the back of the end zone until 1974.

Birthdays: Larry Eisenhauer, 1940; Mark Chmura, 1969; Shawn Jefferson, 1969; Gilbert Brown, 1971; Dhani Jones, 1978; Khalil Mack, 1991

Trivia: In 2015, what kicker became the first player in NFL history to score 1,000 career points with two different teams?

Trivia Answer: Adam Vinatieri (Patriots and Colts)

FEBRUARY

On This Date: On February 23, 1983, Heisman Trophy-winning running back Herschel Walker turned pro after his junior season at Georgia when he signed a three-year deal with the New Jersey Generals of the USFL.

Birthdays: Dante Lavelli, 1923; Tom Osborne, 1937; Jackie Smith, 1940; Fred Biletnikoff, 1943; Ed Flanagan, 1944; Ed "Too Tall" Jones, 1951; Charles Tillman, 1981; Jerod Mayo, 1986; Byron Maxwell, 1988

Trivia: What world-famous figure was an owner of the New Jersey Generals?

Trivia Answer: Donald Trump

FEBRUARY

On This Date: On February 24, 1985, Jim Kelly of the USFL's Houston Gamblers set a pro football record, passing for 574 yards in a win over Steve Young and the Los Angeles Express. Kelly's throwing exhibition also included five touchdown passes.

Birthdays: Lynn Chandnois, 1925; Fred Dean, 1952; Jeff Garcia, 1970; Simeon Rice, 1974; Bob Sanders, 1981; Dwayne Allen, 1990

Trivia: In 2012, who broke Johnny Unitas' long-standing record when he threw a touchdown pass in a 48th consecutive game?

Trivia Answer: Drew Brees

FEBRUARY

On This Date: On February 25, 1989, Jerry Jones, who made his money in the oil and gas exploration business, bought the Dallas Cowboys. Jones became a hands-on owner, naming himself general manager of the team, and remains a visible presence at Cowboys home games.

Birthdays: Bert Bell, 1895; Art Powell, 1937; Jim Tyrer, 1939; Carl Eller, 1942; James Brown, 1951; Jeff Fisher, 1958; Don Majkowski, 1964; Gerald McCoy, 1988; Christian Ponder, 1988

Trivia: Jimmy Johnson and Jerry Jones were college teammates on what 1964 National Championship winner?

Trivia Answer: Arkansas

FEBRUARY

On This Date: On February 26, 1989, Tom Landry was fired as the head coach of the Dallas Cowboys. Landry had been with the team for 29 years, leading the franchise to two Super Bowl titles. The move came one day after Jerry Jones took over in Dallas.

Birthdays: Phil Villapiano, 1949; Wesley Walls, 1966; Marshall Faulk, 1973; Robert Mathis, 1981

Trivia: After Tom Landry, who has had the second-longest tenure as head coach of the Cowboys?

Trivia Answer: Jason Garrett

FEBRUARY

On This Date: On February 27, 2013, the 49ers agreed to trade quarterback Alex Smith to the Chiefs for what ended up being two second round picks. Smith, the #1 pick in 2005, had been given the boot in San Francisco in favor of Colin Kaepernick.

Birthdays: Raymond Berry, 1933; Duce Staley, 1975; Tony Gonzalez, 1976; Chandler Jones, 1990

Trivia: For what NFL team did former 49ers hero Dwight Clark serve as the general manager from the late 1990s to the early 2000s?

Trivia Answer: Cleveland Browns

FEBRUARY

On This Date: On February 28, 1959, the Chicago Cardinals traded future Hall of Fame running back Ollie Matson to the Rams for nine players.

Birthdays: Bubba Smith, 1945; Brian Billick, 1954; Ickey Woods, 1966; Gary Walker, 1973; Carlos Dunlap, 1989

Trivia: In a lopsided trade, the Cowboys received numerous franchise-building picks when they dealt Herschel Walker to what team in 1989?

Trivia Answer: Minnesota Vikings

FEBRUARY

On This Date: On February 29, 2004, the Bowl Championship Series announced it would be adding a fifth bowl in addition to the Orange, Sugar, Fiesta and Rose Bowl games. The first BCS National Championship Game would take place following the 2006 season. (The BCS era, of course, came to an end in 2014.)

Birthdays: John Niland, 1944; Bryce Paup, 1968; Eric Kendricks, 1992

Trivia: Despite a historic performance from QB Deshaun Watson, Clemson lost for the first time all season in the 2016 National Championship Game to what school?

Trivia Answer: Alabama, 45-40

MARCH

On This Date: On March 1, 1941, Elmer Layden, one of Notre Dame's "Four Horsemen," and a former Notre Dame football coach, was named the NFL's first commissioner.

Birthdays: Pete Rozelle, 1926; Elvin Bethea, 1946; Riley Odoms, 1950; Thomas "Hollywood" Henderson, 1953; Mike Rozier, 1961; Stephen Davis, 1974; Tyreek Hill, 1994

Trivia: In the 1993 movie *Rudy*, who stars as Rudy Ruettiger, a small football player who overcomes the odds to play in a college game for Notre Dame?

Trivia Answer: Sean Astin

MARCH

On This Date: On March 2, 1982, Ben Roethlisberger was born. Big Ben made an immediate impact on the NFL and remains the youngest QB to win a Super Bowl (XL). The certain to be Hall of Famer holds Steeler records in numerous passing categories, including the most QB starts and the most wins in team history.

Birthdays: Bill Maas, 1962; Sebastian Janikowski, 1978; Ben Roethlisberger, 1982; Reggie Bush, 1985; Malcolm Butler, 1990

Trivia: What former college quarterback caught the first touchdown pass of Ben Roethlisberger's NFL career?

Trivia Answer: Antwaan Randle El

MARCH

On This Date: On March 3, 1950, the NFL name was restored. The league had traded as the National-American Football League for about three months.

Birthdays: Randy Gradishar, 1952; Herschel Walker, 1962; Santonio Holmes, 1984

Trivia: Former Vikings Pro Bowl receiver and sportscaster Ahmad Rashad originally went by what name?

Trivia Answer: Bobby Moore

MARCH

On This Date: On March 4, 2004, a rare swap of stars occurred when the Denver Broncos traded Pro Bowl running back Clinton Portis to the Washington Redskins for cornerback Champ Bailey and a second round draft pick.

Birthdays: Knute Rockne, 1888; Don Perkins, 1938; Doug Plank, 1953; Shane Conlan, 1964; Jay Gruden, 1967; Robert Smith, 1972

Trivia: The Eagles and Rams pulled off a deal in 2015 that resulted in what two starting quarterbacks switching cities?

Trivia Answer: St. Louis dealt Sam Bradford to Philly for Nick Foles.

MARCH

On This Date: On March 5, 1984, Brigham Young quarterback Steve Young signed a $42 million contract with the Los Angeles Express of the USFL. Unfortunately, the league folded later that year. Fortunately, for Young, his contract was guaranteed.

Birthdays: Fred Williamson, 1937; Rocky Bleier, 1946; Mike Munchak, 1960; Michael Irvin, 1966; Roman Phifer, 1968

Trivia: In 2009, who became the first defensive player in NFL history to sign a $100 million contract?

Trivia Answer: Albert Haynesworth

MARCH

On This Date: On March 6, 2005, the Arizona Cardinals signed quarterback Kurt Warner. Warner, a Super Bowl and regular season MVP for the Rams, had played the previous year with the Giants. The future Hall of Famer resurrected his career in Arizona, where he nearly led his team to a Super Bowl XLIII title before losing a heartbreaker to the Steelers.

Birthdays: Dan Towler, 1928; Bob Trumpy, 1945; Robbie Tobeck, 1970; Andre Gurode, 1978

Trivia: With two sacks and a forced fumble in Super Bowl XLIII against Arizona, what Steeler established a new postseason record with four straight multi-sack games?

Trivia Answer: Lamarr Woodley

MARCH

On This Date: On March 7, 2016, Peyton Manning announced his retirement from the NFL. The Sheriff retired as the league's all-time leader in passing yardage and touchdowns.

Birthdays: Franco Harris, 1950; Lynn Swann, 1952; Tommy Kramer, 1955; Flipper Anderson, 1965; Steve Beuerlein, 1965; Jeff Feagles, 1966; Ricky Proehl, 1968; Sam Gash, 1969

Trivia: In his final NFL game, Peyton Manning failed to throw a touchdown pass. Who was the only Bronco to score an offensive touchdown in Super Bowl 50?

Trivia Answer: C.J. Anderson

MARCH

On This Date: On March 8, 1998, Ray Nitschke died at the age of 61 after suffering a heart attack. Nitschke remains a central figure in Packers lore, winning five championships, including two Super Bowls, with Green Bay. The Hall of Fame linebacker's #66 was retired by the Pack in 1983.

Birthdays: Pete Dawkins, 1938; William Fuller, 1962; Jason Elam, 1970; Hines Ward, 1976

Trivia: In 2005, what Packer became the first player in NFL history to have his number officially retired by two teams?

Trivia Answer: Reggie White, #92, who was also honored by the Eagles

MARCH

On This Date: On March 9, 2014, William Clay Ford, the owner of the Lions, died at age 88. Just 16 days later, Ralph Wilson, who had been in charge of the Bills, died at 95. As a result, the NFL wound up losing its two longest-tenured owners in a matter of weeks.

Birthdays: Tom Sestak, 1936; Dennis Harrah, 1953; Mark Dantonio, 1956; Sean Salisbury, 1963; Brian Bosworth, 1965; Antonio Bryant, 1981

Trivia: Who's the only female owner to have a Super Bowl championship team?

Trivia Answer: Georgia Frontiere, with the Rams

MARCH

On This Date: On March 10, 1965, Rod Woodson was born. The all-time great defensive back was the 1993 Defensive Player of the Year, was named to the NFL's 1990s All-Decade Team, and won a Super Bowl in three appearances.

Birthdays: Bulldog Turner, 1919; Ron Mix, 1938; Joe Bugel, 1940; Curley Culp, 1946; Rod Woodson, 1965; Logan Mankins, 1982; Martellus Bennett, 1987

Trivia: In 2004, the excessive jamming of receivers by cornerbacks led the NFL to place more emphasis on a rule first named after what Steelers Hall of Famer?

Trivia Answer: Mel Blount

MARCH

On This Date: On March 11, 1986, the NFL adopted an instant replay system to review disputed calls following a vote by league owners. After abandoning the idea six years later, the system would return for the 1999 season.

Birthdays: Shawn Springs, 1975; Lee Evans, 1981; Greg Olsen, 1985

Trivia: Playing By The Rules: A defensive player intercepts a pass in his own end zone. He attempts to run it out but is tackled in the end zone. What is the ruling?

Trivia Answer: Touchback

MARCH

On This Date: On March 12, 1987, legendary coach Woody Hayes died. Hayes won five National Championships and 13 Big Ten titles during his 28-year tenure at Ohio State.

Birthdays: Mark Moseley, 1948; Matt Millen, 1958; Merton Hanks, 1968; Shaun Rogers, 1979; Dont'a Hightower, 1990

Trivia: Before he entered the professional ranks to lead the Browns, what legend coached Ohio State to their first football title in 1942?

Trivia Answer: Paul Brown

MARCH

On This Date: On March 13, 2000, Dan Marino officially announced his retirement from the National Football League. Marino, a nine-time Pro Bowler and the 1984 MVP, was the first NFL quarterback to throw for 5,000 yards in a season.

Birthdays: Sherrill Headrick, 1937; Trent Dilfer, 1972; Dan Wilkinson, 1973; Marcell Dareus, 1990

Trivia: In his lone championship appearance, Dan Marino had 318 yards passing as his Dolphins lost to what team in Super Bowl XIX?

Trivia Answer: San Francisco 49ers, 38-16

MARCH

On This Date: On March 14, 1967, in preparation for their merger, the AFL and NFL held their first combined draft. The Baltimore Colts chose Michigan State defensive lineman Bubba Smith with the first pick.

Birthdays: Antowain Smith, 1972; Ron Dayne, 1978; Daryl Smith, 1982; Ahmad Brooks, 1984

Trivia: One of the biggest draft busts ever, what Michigan State product was tabbed by *Sports Illustrated* as "the best offensive line prospect ever" before Green Bay took him #2 in 1989?

Trivia Answer: Tony Mandarich

MARCH

On This Date: On March 15, 1926, Norm Van
Brocklin was born. Van Brocklin, a fourth round draft pick in
1949, went to the Pro Bowl nine times and set a record for the
most passing yards in a game with 554 for the Rams in 1951.

Birthdays: Norm Van Brocklin, 1926; Ted Marchibroda, 1931;
Rick Volk, 1945; Clay Matthews Jr., 1956; Mike Tomlin, 1972;
Eric Decker, 1987; Tavon Austin, 1991; Devonta Freeman, 1992

Trivia: True or False? Kurt Warner, with the Rams and
Cardinals, has posted the three highest Super Bowl single-game
passing yardage totals.

Trivia Answer: False - He had, until Tom Brady threw for 466 yards in Super Bowl LI.

MARCH

On This Date: On March 16, 1964, Paul
Hornung and Alex Karras were reinstated by the NFL
after being suspended 11 months earlier for gambling on
football games.

Birthdays: Joe DeLamielleure, 1951; Ozzie Newsome, 1956;
Mel Gray, 1961; Rodney Peete, 1966; Todd Heap, 1980;
Tramon Williams, 1983

Trivia: What Super Bowl-related activity resulted in the NFL
handing out a $100,000 fine to Mike Tice in 2005?

*Trivia Answer: He was found guilty of organizing and profiting from a Super Bowl ticket
scalping operation.*

MARCH

On This Date: On March 17, 1994, an announcement was made that Phoenix would change its name to the Arizona Cardinals, thus enhancing statewide promotion.

Birthdays: Sonny Werblin, 1910; Sammy Baugh, 1914; Chuck Muncie, 1953; Emmanuel Sanders, 1987; Cordarrelle Patterson, 1991

Trivia: What NFL team was named after an Edgar Allan Poe poem?

Trivia Answer: Baltimore Ravens (The Raven)

MARCH

On This Date: On March 18, 2006, the Cowboys signed talented, but controversial All-Pro wide receiver Terrell Owens. Even in his mid-30s, Owens would gain 1,000 yards and catch double-digit touchdown passes in each of his three seasons in Dallas.

Birthdays: Benny Friedman, 1905; Mike Webster, 1952; Curt Warner, 1961; Keith Millard, 1962; Andre Rison, 1967; Brian Griese, 1975; Travis Frederick, 1991; Anthony Barr, 1992

Trivia: After scoring in a game at Cleveland in 2007, what colorful receiver made good on his promise by leaping into the Dawg Pound?

Trivia Answer: Chad Johnson

MARCH

On This Date: On March 19, 1991, the NFL voted to move Super Bowl XXVII from Tempe, Arizona, to the Pasadena Rose Bowl. The decision to strip Arizona of the 1993 Super Bowl was due to the state not recognizing Martin Luther King Jr. Day.

Birthdays: Jay Berwanger, 1914; Charley Hennigan, 1935; Joe Kapp, 1938; Andy Reid, 1958; Steve Gleason, 1977; EJ Manuel, 1990

Trivia: In Super Bowl XXVII, this showboating Cowboy, nearing the end zone on a fumble recovery, was caught from behind just shy of the goal line and lost the ball for a Buffalo touchback. Who is he?

Trivia Answer: Leon Lett

MARCH

On This Date: On March 20, 2006, Paul Tagliabue, after a 16-year reign, announced that he would retire as Commissioner of the NFL later in the year. Roger Goodell would take over during the summer.

Birthdays: Karl Kassulke, 1941; Rickey Jackson, 1958; Marcus Vick, 1984

Trivia: What six-year Texans tackle was elected President of the National Football League Players Association in March of 2014?

Trivia Answer: Eric Winston

MARCH

On This Date: On March 21, 1946, Kenny Washington became the first black athlete in the NFL when he signed with the Los Angeles Rams. The milestone came a full year before Jackie Robinson broke baseball's color barrier with the Dodgers.

Birthdays: Tom Flores, 1937; Dick Schafrath, 1937; Jay Hilgenberg, 1959; Adrian Peterson, 1985; Jonathan Stewart, 1987

Trivia: In the late-1940s, the Rams became the first pro football team to have an emblem on their helmets. What was it?

Trivia Answer: Horns

MARCH

On This Date: On March 22, 1989, Pete Rozelle announced his retirement as commissioner of the NFL. It was during Rozelle's tenure that the NFL became hugely popular with the creation of the Super Bowl and huge television contracts which expanded the league's growth tremendously.

Birthdays: Jimbo Covert, 1960; Russell Maryland, 1969; Joey Porter, 1977; Thomas Davis, 1983; Chris Ivory, 1988; J.J. Watt, 1989

Trivia: If the Pete Rozelle Trophy, given to the Super Bowl MVP, was engraved with the former commissioner's actual first name, what would it be called?

Trivia Answer: The Alvin Rozelle Trophy

MARCH

On This Date: On March 23, 1991, the NFL launched the World League of American Football (later re-named NFL Europe) to become the first league to operate on a weekly basis on two separate continents.

Birthdays: Ron Jaworski, 1951; Carl Pickens, 1970; Jeremy Newberry, 1976; Brandon Marshall, 1984; Maurice Jones-Drew, 1985

Trivia: In 2007, where did the Giants and Dolphins play the first ever regular season NFL game outside of North America?

Trivia Answer: London's Wembley Stadium (The Giants won, 13-10.)

MARCH

On This Date: On March 24, 1988, quarterback Dan Fouts officially called it quits after 15 years with the San Diego Chargers. With that came this quip - "Now that I'm retired, I want to say that all defensive linemen are sissies."

Birthdays: Larry Wilson, 1938; Vaughan Johnson, 1962; Mike Vanderjagt, 1970; Aaron Brooks, 1976; Peyton Manning, 1976

Trivia: What Chargers head coach had stints as an NFL Europe quarterback for the Amsterdam Admirals and a CFL QB for the Calgary Stampeders in the late 1990s?

Trivia Answer: Mike McCoy

MARCH

On This Date: On March 25, 1971, Boston changed its name to the New England Patriots. The team had been known as the "Boston Patriots" since its inception in the AFL in 1960.

Birthdays: Howard Cosell, 1918; Rulon Jones, 1958; Fred Robbins, 1977

Trivia: What Patriot and 1964 American Football League MVP is the all-time leading scorer in the league's history?

Trivia Answer: Gino Cappelletti

MARCH

On This Date: On March 26, 2003, the Arizona Cardinals signed former Cowboys running back Emmitt Smith. Smith, the league's all-time rushing leader, would play his last two seasons in Arizona before signing a one-day contract with Dallas to retire a Cowboy.

Birthdays: Gino Cappelletti, 1934; Marcus Allen, 1960; Devery Henderson, 1982; Rashad Jennings, 1985; DeAndre Levy, 1987; Von Miller, 1989

Trivia: Emmitt Smith won the third season of what reality TV show in 2006?

Trivia Answer: Dancing with the Stars (with partner Cheryl Burke)

MARCH

On This Date: On March 27, 2006, NFL teams unanimously decided to return the name of the official game ball to "The Duke" to honor New York Giants owner Wellington Mara, who died the previous year.

Birthdays: Mike Curtis, 1943; Doug Wilkerson, 1947; Randall Cunningham, 1963; Domonique Foxworth, 1983

Trivia: What sports equipment manufacturer has provided the official game ball of the NFL since 1941?

Trivia Answer: Wilson

MARCH

On This Date: On March 28, 1984, unannounced and in the middle of the night, moving vans loaded with Baltimore Colts equipment made their way out of town and headed for Indianapolis, where the Colts would make their new home.

Birthdays: Joe Fortunato, 1930; Jason Garrett, 1966; Chris Long, 1985; Toby Gerhart, 1987; Geno Atkins, 1988; Derek Carr, 1991

Trivia: Before the Ravens moved into their new digs in 1998, they played their first two NFL seasons in what stadium that housed the Baltimore Colts for 30 years?

Trivia Answer: Memorial Stadium

MARCH

On This Date: On March 29, 1977, a 16-game season, 4-game preseason, and a second wild card team for the playoffs in the 1978 season were all adopted.

Birthdays: Emlen Tunnell, 1925; Earl Campbell, 1955; Brian Jordan, 1967; Chris Calloway, 1968; Adam Gase, 1978; Justin Tuck, 1983; Ryan Kalil, 1985

Trivia: How many teams are there currently in the NFL?

Trivia Answer: 32

MARCH

On This Date: On March 30, 1976, an NFL expansion draft was held for the league's two newest teams, the Seattle Seahawks and Tampa Bay Buccaneers. Each club selected 39 players from the other 26 teams.

Birthdays: Willie Galimore, 1935; Charlie Weis, 1956; Lomas Brown, 1963; Jammal Brown, 1981; Richard Sherman, 1988

Trivia: Before they began play in 1976, the Seahawks made a franchise-altering move by acquiring what player from the Houston Oilers for an eighth round draft pick?

Trivia Answer: Steve Largent

MARCH

On This Date: On March 31, 1931, a plane crash in Kansas claimed the life of Notre Dame football coach Knute Rockne at the age of 43. During his 13 years with the Irish, Rockne posted the highest all-time winning percentage (.881) for a major college gridiron coach, including five undefeated seasons without a tie.

Birthdays: Jimmy Johnson, 1938; Ed Marinaro, 1950; Mark Tuinei, 1960; John Taylor, 1962; Steve Smith, 1969; James Jones, 1984

Trivia: Lou Holtz's only head coaching job in the NFL was with what team?

Trivia Answer: New York Jets, in 1976

APRIL

On This Date: On April 1, 1983, Sean Taylor was born. The hard-hitting Redskins safety made an immediate impact on the NFL, earning two Pro Bowl nods in four seasons. His life would be cut short at the age of 24 when he succumbed to injuries from a gunshot wound after his Miami home was broken into.

Birthdays: Bo Schembechler, 1929; Jumbo Elliott, 1965; Sean Taylor, 1983

Trivia: What Redskins Super Bowl safety became the head coach of the New York Jets in 2015?

Trivia Answer: Todd Bowles

APRIL

On This Date: On April 2, 1995, Lawrence Taylor defeated Bam Bam Bigelow in the main event at Wrestlemania XI in Hartford, Connecticut.

Birthdays: Arnie Herber, 1910; Roy Gerela, 1948; Bill Romanowski, 1966

Trivia: Dwayne "The Rock" Johnson was a college football player who won a national championship as a member of what 1991 team?

Trivia Answer: University of Miami Hurricanes

APRIL

On This Date: On April 3, 2007, legendary coach Eddie Robinson died at 88. With Grambling, Robinson won 408 games in 55 seasons at the helm. He was inducted into the College Football Hall of Fame in 1997, the year he retired.

Birthdays: Jim Parker, 1934; Lyle Alzado, 1949; Russ Francis, 1953; Mike Pruitt, 1954; Leslie Frazier, 1959; Rodney Hampton, 1969; Jared Allen, 1982; Kam Chancellor, 1988; John Brown, 1990

Trivia: Coach Tom Coughlin played in the same backfield with Floyd Little and Larry Csonka at what college?

Trivia Answer: Syracuse University

APRIL

On This Date: On April 4, 1951, John Hannah was born in Canton, Georgia. He would be enshrined in Pro Football's Hall of Fame in Canton, Ohio, 40 years later. Hannah, a College Hall of Famer as well, was renowned as a premier guard for the Patriots and was an All-Pro from 1976-85.

Birthdays: Ed White, 1947; John Hannah, 1951; Tom Jackson, 1951; Jack Del Rio, 1963; Jessie Tuggle, 1965; Keith Bulluck, 1977

Trivia: The Pro Football Hall of Fame is located in Canton, Ohio, on what street?

Trivia Answer: George Halas Drive

APRIL

On This Date: On April 5, 1973, the NFL's first jersey numbering system was adopted. 1-19 was used for quarterbacks and specialists, 20-49 for running backs and defensive backs, 50-59 for centers and linebackers, 60-79 for defensive linemen and non-center offensive linemen, and 80-89 for tight ends and wide receivers.

Birthdays: Glenn "Pop" Warner, 1871; Jon Morris, 1942; Brad Van Pelt, 1951; Dwight Hicks, 1956; Tony Banks, 1973; Marc Bulger, 1977

Trivia: In nine straight Super Bowls (VI to XIV), the starting quarterback for the winning team wore the same uniform number. What?

Trivia Answer: 12

APRIL

On This Date: On April 6, 1997, Jack Kent Cooke died. Cooke, who started out as an encyclopedia salesman, owned the Washington Redskins, the Los Angeles Lakers of the NBA, and the Los Angeles Kings of the NHL.

Birthdays: Spider Lockhart, 1943; Bill Brooks, 1964; Sterling Sharpe, 1965; Donnie Edwards, 1973; Tim Hasselbeck, 1978

Trivia: The Seahawks were the second pro sports team purchased by Paul Allen. What NBA franchise did he take charge of in the late 1980s?

Trivia Answer: Portland Trail Blazers

APRIL

On This Date: On April 7, 1943, the NFL made helmets mandatory and adopted a 10-game season for all teams.

Birthdays: Tony Dorsett, 1954; Steve Wisniewski, 1967; Ricky Watters, 1969; Ronde & Tiki Barber, 1975; Dominique Rodgers-Cromartie, 1986; Jared Cook, 1987

Trivia: What inventor of basketball is often credited with introducing helmets to the game of football?

Trivia Answer: Dr. James Naismith

APRIL

On This Date: On April 8, 1966, 36-year-old Al Davis was chosen as the AFL's new commissioner after Joe Foss resigned.

Birthdays: Miller Farr, 1943; Ricky Bell, 1955; Fred Smerlas, 1957; Mark Clayton, 1961; Cliff Avril, 1986

Trivia: True or False? In his first year as an AFL head coach, 1963, Al Davis led Oakland to a 1-13 record.

Trivia Answer: False - Davis was the AFL Coach of the Year after taking the Raiders to 10-4. The team had gone 1-13 the previous season.

APRIL

On This Date: On April 9, 1898, Curly Lambeau was born. Lambeau founded the pre-NFL Packers in 1919, was the coach-general manager of the team until 1949, and is credited with keeping pro football alive in Green Bay. His 30+ years of coaching yielded six championships with the Packers.

Birthdays: Curly Lambeau, 1898; Clarence Scott, 1949; Willie Colon, 1983

Trivia: What Packers defensive back was credited with starting the Lambeau Leap in 1993?

Trivia Answer: LeRoy Butler

APRIL

On This Date: On April 10, 1995, the NFL became the first sports league to establish its own website. Today, you can visit it at, very simply, NFL.com.

Birthdays: Clarke Hinkle, 1909; John Madden, 1936; Don Meredith, 1938; Mike Stratton, 1941; Mel Blount, 1948; Steve Tasker, 1962; Kirk Lowdermilk, 1963; Neil Smith, 1966; Kareem Jackson, 1988

Trivia: What year did the NFL Network launch: 2003, 2005 or 2007?

Trivia Answer: 2003

APRIL

On This Date: On April 11, 2010, Texas Stadium, the home of the Dallas Cowboys for nearly 40 years, was demolished. America's Team had moved into their new $1.3 billion stadium the previous year.

Birthdays: Danny Fortmann, 1916; Houston Antwine, 1939; Louis Vasquez, 1987

Trivia: For what non-football sporting event in 2010 did the new Cowboys Stadium have over 108,000 fans in attendance?

Trivia Answer: The NBA All-Star Game

APRIL

On This Date: On April 12, 1995, the NFL
approved the move of the Los Angeles Rams to St. Louis.
The league would go without a franchise in Los Angeles for two
decades, until the Rams returned to L.A. for the 2016 season.

Birthdays: Tom Addison, 1936; Mike Garrett, 1944;
Charles Mann, 1961; Lorenzo White, 1966; Michael Jackson, 1969;
Ted Ginn Jr., 1985

Trivia: What current NFL team briefly called Los Angeles its
home during its AFL days in the 1960s?

Trivia Answer: The Los Angeles Chargers

APRIL

On This Date: On April 13, 1970, Commissioner
Pete Rozelle awarded the Miami Dolphins' first round draft
selection to the Baltimore Colts. The Colts received the pick as
compensation for Don Shula (the former Baltimore coach), who
accepted the top job on the field for the Dolphins.

Birthdays: Ted Washington, 1968; Josh Gordon, 1991;
Melvin Gordon, 1993

Trivia: Who is the only man to be the head coach of both the
Baltimore Colts and Baltimore Ravens?

Trivia Answer: Ted Marchibroda

APRIL

On This Date: On April 14, 2016, the Titans dealt the first pick in the upcoming draft to the Rams in a blockbuster deal that involved L.A. giving up two first and two second-round picks. The Rams would take Cal QB Jared Goff #1.

Birthdays: Joe Kuharich, 1917; Stan Humphries, 1965; Max Unger, 1986; Joe Haden, 1989

Trivia: What team received a wealth of draft choices when they moved out of the #2 spot of the 2012 NFL Draft after the Redskins traded up to select Robert Griffin III?

Trivia Answer: St. Louis Rams

APRIL

On This Date: On April 15, 2015, Aaron Hernandez was found guilty of first-degree murder in the shooting death of Odin Lloyd. The former Patriots tight end is currently serving a sentence of life in prison without the possibility of parole.

Birthdays: Anthony Miller, 1965; Jason Sehorn, 1971; Antonio Cromartie, 1984

Trivia: The last time the Patriots took a tight end in the first round of the NFL Draft, 2004, they chose a man who scored a reported 48 out of 50 on the Wonderlic Test. Who?

Trivia Answer: Ben Watson

APRIL

On This Date: On April 16, 2000, the New England Patriots used their sixth round draft choice to select Michigan's Tom Brady. Six quarterbacks were chosen before the all-time great, who was taken with the 199th overall pick.

Birthdays: Dick "Night Train" Lane, 1928; Bill Belichick, 1952; Steve Emtman, 1970; Jonathan Vilma, 1982; Johnathan Joseph, 1984; Joe McKnight, 1988; Tevin Coleman, 1993

Trivia: In 2001, what Pro Bowl wideout caught the first touchdown pass of Tom Brady's NFL career?

Trivia Answer: Terry Glenn

APRIL

On This Date: On April 17, 1999, five quarterbacks were selected within the first 12 picks of the NFL Draft. Tim Couch of Kentucky went number one to the Browns, followed by Donovan McNabb, Akili Smith, Daunte Culpepper and Cade McNown.

Birthdays: Delvin Williams, 1951; Boomer Esiason, 1961; Tony Boselli, 1972

Trivia: With 26, two players hold the NFL mark for the most touchdown passes thrown by a rookie quarterback. The years were 1998 and 2012. Name the QBs.

Trivia Answer: Peyton Manning and Russell Wilson

APRIL

18

On This Date: On April 18, 1995, legendary quarterback Joe Montana retired. Joe Cool led the San Francisco 49ers to four Super Bowl championships, and was named the MVP in three of them. He also won two league MVP awards, and was inducted into the Hall of Fame in 2000.

Birthdays: Richie Petitbon, 1938; Walt Sweeney, 1941; Pete Gogolak, 1942; Eric Wright, 1959; Wilbur Marshall, 1962; Willie Roaf, 1970; Derrick Brooks, 1973

Trivia: As a member of the 1984 49ers, what Pro Bowl lineman and shot putter is the only athlete to win both a Super Bowl ring and an Olympic medal within a year's time?

Trivia Answer: Michael Carter

APRIL

19

On This Date: On April 19, 1997, future Hall of Famer Orlando Pace was selected #1 overall by the St. Louis Rams in the NFL Draft. Another Hall of Fame tackle, Walter Jones, would be taken just five picks later by the Seahawks.

Birthdays: Jack Pardee, 1936; Harris Barton, 1964; Keith Jackson, 1965; Aaron Smith, 1976; Troy Polamalu, 1981

Trivia: What offensive lineman became the first pick in the history of the Ravens when Baltimore selected him #4 overall in the 1996 NFL Draft?

Trivia Answer: Jonathan Ogden

APRIL

On This Date: On April 20, 2002, the Houston Texans took part in their first-ever NFL Draft. They used the first overall pick on quarterback David Carr, who would have a rough go of it in his rookie year. He was sacked a record 76 times.

Birthdays: Ernie Stautner, 1925; George Andrie, 1940; Steve Spurrier, 1945; John Carney, 1964; Luke Kuechly, 1991

Trivia: What team sacked Jay Cutler nine times in the first half in an embarrassing 2010 Chicago defeat?

Trivia Answer: New York Giants

APRIL

On This Date: On April 21, 2001, the Atlanta Falcons selected electrifying Virginia Tech quarterback Michael Vick with the first overall pick in the NFL Draft. The Chargers, who traded out of the #1 spot, would make out as the real winners, as they grabbed Hall of Famer LaDainian Tomlinson at #5.

Birthdays: Steve Owen, 1898; Ken Strong, 1906; Tony Romo, 1980; Cadillac Williams, 1982; Tarvaris Jackson, 1983

Trivia: Back in 1995, who was the last running back to be selected #1 overall in the NFL Draft?

Trivia Answer: Ki-Jana Carter, to the Bengals

APRIL

On This Date: On April 22, 2004, former Cardinals safety Pat Tillman lost his life while serving his country in Afghanistan. Tillman, a College Football Hall of Famer, turned down a multi-million dollar contract from Arizona to enlist in the U.S. Army in 2002.

Birthdays: Freeman McNeil, 1959; Jeff Hostetler, 1961; Marshawn Lynch, 1986; Kenny Stills, 1992

Trivia: What United States Army Captain made his NFL debut with the Steelers at left tackle during the 2015 season?

Trivia Answer: Alejandro Villanueva

APRIL

On This Date: On April 23, 2005, the San Francisco 49ers looked to return to the glory days when they drafted quarterback Alex Smith with the first overall pick. The Niners passed on Aaron Rodgers, who fell all the way to #24 and into the lap of Green Bay.

Birthdays: Bud Wilkinson, 1916; Joe Ferguson, 1950; Sam Madison, 1974; Kyle Juszczyk, 1991; Jake Fisher, 1993

Trivia: What historic bust went #1 in the 2007 NFL Draft before the Lions selected Calvin Johnson #2?

Trivia Answer: JaMarcus Russell, to the Raiders

APRIL

On This Date: On April 24, 2004, the San Diego Chargers selected an unhappy Eli Manning first overall in the NFL Draft before dealing him to the New York Giants. Future stars Larry Fitzgerald, Philip Rivers and Ben Roethlisberger would also be chosen within the next ten picks.

Birthdays: Mike Michalske, 1903; Carroll Dale, 1938; Bob Chandler, 1949; Vince Ferragamo, 1954

Trivia: In the 2004 NFL Draft, what school set a new record by having six of its players drafted in the first round?

Trivia Answer: University of Miami

APRIL

On This Date: On April 25, 2016, the 2nd U.S. Circuit Court of Appeals reinstated Tom Brady's four-game suspension for the 2016 regular season stemming from "Deflategate". Two months later, Brady announced that he would not appeal any further and would accept the suspension.

Birthdays: Randy Cross, 1954; Joe Buck, 1969; Darren Woodson, 1969; DeAngelo Williams, 1983; Lamar Miller, 1991

Trivia: Tom Brady's final game at the University of Michigan was a thriller. He threw four TDs as the Wolverines beat Alabama in overtime, 35-34, in what 2000 bowl game?

Trivia Answer: Orange Bowl

APRIL

On This Date: On April 26, 2012, the Colts selected Andrew Luck in the NFL Draft. Exactly 29 years earlier, they took another quarterback #1 overall, but he would never play a game for the franchise. His name? John Elway.

Birthdays: Steve Nelson, 1951; Natrone Means, 1972; Marco Rivera, 1972; Mike McKenzie, 1976; Cole Beasley, 1989

Trivia: What Hall of Fame quarterback was drafted by the Steelers in 1955 but cut before the season even began?

Trivia Answer: Johnny Unitas

APRIL

On This Date: On April 27, 1982, the Raiders selected USC Heisman Trophy-winning running back Marcus Allen with the 10th pick in the NFL Draft. Allen would go on to win the Rookie of the Year Award and was named the Super Bowl MVP in 1984.

Birthdays: Chuck Knox, 1932; Lee Roy Jordan, 1941; Herman Edwards, 1954; Donald Penn, 1983; Keenan Allen, 1992

Trivia: Who topped Marcus Allen by a yard to break the record for the longest run from scrimmage in Super Bowl history?

Trivia Answer: Willie Parker, who ran 75 yards for a score in Pittsburgh's win over Seattle in Super Bowl XL)

APRIL

On This Date: On April 28, 1981, the New Orleans Saints passed on Lawrence Taylor with the first pick in the NFL Draft. Instead, they took Heisman Trophy winner George Rogers. The Giants then took Taylor and the rest is history.

Birthdays: Mark Bavaro, 1963; Mark Carrier, 1968; Jamal Williams, 1976; Scott Fujita, 1979; Blake Bortles, 1992

Trivia: In 1981, George Rogers and Lawrence Taylor became the first #1 and #2 NFL Draft choices to win the Offensive and Defensive Rookie of the Year awards. Who became the second pair in 2010?

Trivia Answer: #1 pick Sam Bradford (Offensive ROY) and #2 pick Ndamukong Suh (Defensive ROY)

APRIL

On This Date: On April 29, 2006, the Houston Texans surprised many when they made NC State defensive end Mario Williams the first overall pick in the NFL Draft. Heisman winner Reggie Bush went #2.

Birthdays: George Allen, 1918; Jim Hart, 1944; Jay Cutler, 1983; Tommie Harris, 1983

Trivia: From 2001-12, only two non-quarterbacks were drafted #1 overall. Mario Williams was one. In 2008, who was the other?

Trivia Answer: Jake Long (Dolphins)

APRIL

On This Date: On April 30, 1996, NFL owners approved the Houston Oilers' move to Nashville. The Oilers would move to Tennessee for the 1997 season and become the Titans in 1999.

Birthdays: Jerry Stovall, 1941; Al Toon, 1963; Dave Meggett, 1966

Trivia: The New York Titans began play in 1960, and have been known since 1963 as...what?

Trivia Answer: New York Jets

MAY

On This Date: On May 1, 1984, the New York Giants took Michigan State linebacker Carl Banks with the third overall pick in the NFL Draft. Banks would team with Lawrence Taylor to form one of the best linebacking duos of all-time and help lead the Giants to Super Bowl titles in 1986 and 1990.

Birthdays: Chuck Bednarik, 1925; Ollie Matson, 1930; Roger Brown, 1937; Gary Clark, 1962; Curtis Martin, 1973; Wes Welker, 1981; Bradley Roby, 1992

Trivia: He was a linebacker for the New York Giants his entire career (1976-1988) and was inducted into the Pro Football Hall of Fame in 2006. Who is he?

Trivia Answer: Harry Carson

MAY

On This Date: On May 2, 1984, the Dallas Cowboys drafted track legend Carl Lewis as a wide receiver in the 12th round. Lewis would never play a down in the NFL.

Birthdays: Russ Grimm, 1959; Marc Mariani, 1987; Pat McAfee, 1987

Trivia: Who was the last wide receiver to go #1 overall in the NFL Draft?

Trivia Answer: Keyshawn Johnson, to the Jets in 1996

MAY

On This Date: On May 3, 1979, the San Diego Chargers selected Missouri tight end Kellen Winslow with the 13th pick in the NFL Draft. Winslow would redefine the position of tight end and was elected to the Hall of Fame in 1995.

Birthdays: Dave Robinson, 1941; Greg Gumbel, 1946; Erik McMillan, 1965; Joseph Addai, 1983; Jerick McKinnon, 1992

Trivia: To move up one spot and get the #2 pick in the 1998 NFL Draft, the Chargers dealt the Cardinals their #3 and #33 picks, a 1999 first rounder, and Pro Bowler Eric Metcalf. Who did San Diego select?

Trivia Answer: Ryan Leaf

MAY

On This Date: On May 4, 1979, the St. Louis Cardinals selected Michigan State All-American wide receiver Kirk Gibson in the seventh round of the NFL Draft. Instead, the multi-talented Gibson went on to a baseball career, playing on World Series winners with the Detroit Tigers and Los Angeles Dodgers, contributing historic home runs in the process.

Birthdays: Elmer Layden, 1903; Harlon Hill, 1932; Rohn Stark, 1959; Eugene Daniel, 1961; James Harrison, 1978

Trivia: He played in the College World Series at Michigan State and was a Super Bowl-winning quarterback who later became a QB coach at the University of Miami in the late '70s. Who is he?

Trivia Answer: Earl Morrall

MAY

On This Date: On May 5, 1941, Terry Baker was born. Baker, an Oregon State quarterback, was the Heisman Trophy winner and *Sports Illustrated's* Sportsman of the Year in 1962. A multi-sport star, Baker is the only athlete to win a Heisman Trophy and play in the Final Four. The Rams made him the #1 pick of the NFL Draft in 1963, but he had an uneventful pro career.

Birthdays: Tony Canadeo, 1919; Terry Baker, 1941; Muhsin Muhammad, 1973; Ike Taylor, 1980; Mike Daniels, 1989

Trivia: In addition to football, Tony Gonzalez was a basketball player who took part in the 1997 Sweet Sixteen of the NCAA Tournament for what school?

Trivia Answer: California

MAY

On This Date: On May 6, 1982, Dallas Cowboys tight end Jason Witten was born. Witten, a surefire future Hall of Famer, has over 1,000 receptions in his career and is considered one of the all-time greats at his position.

Birthdays: Weeb Ewbank, 1907; Pat Harder, 1922; Ken Harvey, 1965; John Abraham, 1978; Akbar Gbaja-Biamila, 1979; Jason Witten, 1982

Trivia: In 1994, what Patriot's 96 receptions were the most ever for a tight end until Tony Gonzalez surpassed him ten years later?

Trivia Answer: Ben Coates

MAY

On This Date: On May 7, 1946, Woody Strode joined UCLA teammate Kenny Washington to become the first African-American players in the NFL in the modern era. Strode signed with the Los Angeles Rams two months after Washington joined the team.

Birthdays: Babe Parilli, 1930; Johnny Unitas, 1933; Pat McInally, 1953; Ronnie Harmon, 1964; Leslie O'Neal, 1964; Alex Smith, 1984; Earl Thomas, 1989

Trivia: When the Giants played the Patriots in Super Bowl XLII, who became the first black referee to be chosen as the head official in a Super Bowl?

Trivia Answer: Mike Carey

MAY

On This Date: On May 8, 2014, the NFL Draft took place in New York City for the 50th consecutive year. The Texans selected Jadeveon Clowney with the first overall pick. The following year's draft would be moved to Chicago.

Birthdays: Doug Atkins, 1930; Bill Cowher, 1957; Lovie Smith, 1958; Ronnie Lott, 1959; Korey Stringer, 1974; Felix Jones, 1987; Lane Johnson, 1990

Trivia: What former New York Yankees draft choice did the Texans select in the sixth round of the 2003 NFL Draft before ultimately dealing him to the Cowboys?

Trivia Answer: Drew Henson

MAY

On This Date: On May 9, 2002, Hall of Fame college football coach Dan Devine died at the age of 77. Devine led the programs at Arizona State and Missouri, and was the head coach of Notre Dame's 1977 national championship team. Before his time with the Irish, he entered the NFL ranks to coach the Packers in the early '70s.

Birthdays: Jesse Whittenton, 1934; Bob Jeter, 1937; Jake Long, 1985

Trivia: In 1974, what school, behind Anthony Davis' four touchdowns, stunned Notre Dame with 55 unanswered points to come from behind and win, 55-24?

Trivia Answer: USC

MAY

On This Date: On May 10, 2014, Michael Sam became the first openly gay player to be drafted by an NFL team. Sam, the 2013 SEC Defensive Player of the Year with Missouri, was selected by the Rams in the seventh round.

Birthdays: Pat Summerall, 1930; Randy Rasmussen, 1945; Jim Zorn, 1953; Chris Berman, 1955; Jabaal Sheard, 1989

Trivia: The 2014 movie *Draft Day* focuses on the fictionalized general manager and war room actions of what NFL team?

Trivia Answer: Cleveland Browns

MAY

On This Date: On May 11, 1982, the United States Football League (USFL) was officially launched and announced that play would begin in the spring of 1983.

Birthdays: Steve Bono, 1962; Matt Leinart, 1983; Jeremy Maclin, 1988; Cam Newton, 1989

Trivia: What Hall of Fame pass rusher played two seasons for the USFL's Memphis Showboats?

Trivia Answer: Reggie White

MAY

On This Date: On May 12, 1977, Joe Namath signed with the Los Angeles Rams. Namath wound up starting just four games for the franchise, making L.A. the final stop of his pro career after 12 years as a Jet.

Birthdays: Max Montoya, 1956; James Wilder, 1958; Lawrence Phillips, 1975; Mike Furrey, 1977; Chris Hovan, 1978; Andre Carter, 1979; Steve Smith, 1979; Mike Iupati, 1987

Trivia: With what team did Mark Sanchez make eight starts in 2014 after spending the first four years of his NFL career with the Jets?

Trivia Answer: Philadelphia Eagles

MAY

On This Date: On May 13, 1983, Bud Grant was elected to the Canadian Football Hall of Fame. The Winnipeg Blue Bombers and Minnesota Vikings head coach would become the first member of both the Pro and Canadian Football Halls when he was inducted to the former in 1994.

Birthdays: Tom Nalen, 1971; L.J. Smith, 1980; Shaun Phillips, 1981; Tyrann Mathieu, 1992

Trivia: Bud Grant is the only man to coach a team in the Super Bowl (Vikings) and play on a championship team in what sport?

Trivia Answer: NBA (Minneapolis Lakers)

MAY

On This Date: On May 14, 1992, Lyle Alzado died of brain cancer at 43. Alzado, an All-Pro defensive lineman, claimed that steroid abuse contributed to his fatal illness.

Birthdays: Mike Quick, 1959; Tony Siragusa, 1967; Frank Gore, 1983; Carl Nicks, 1985; Clay Matthews, 1986; Lawrence Timmons, 1986; Rob Gronkowski, 1989

Trivia: The controversial Brian Bosworth was banned from the 1987 New Year's Day Orange Bowl due to steroid usage. What school did he play for?

Trivia Answer: Oklahoma

MAY

On This Date: On May 15, 1969, 1970 and 1975, three Super Bowl MVPs were born – Emmitt Smith, Desmond Howard and Ray Lewis, respectively. All three, incidentally, have also had TV gigs with ESPN.

Birthdays: Joey Browner, 1960; Emmitt Smith, 1969; Desmond Howard, 1970; Rod Smith, 1970; Ray Lewis, 1975; Ryan Leaf, 1976; Andy Levitre, 1986

Trivia: In their defeat to the Baltimore Colts, what Cowboy became the first defensive player, and the first from a losing team, to be named the Super Bowl MVP?

Trivia Answer: Chuck Howley

MAY

16

On This Date: On May 16, 1966, the NFL moved the field goal posts to the goal line, painted them bright yellow, and set the uprights 20 feet above the crossbar. (Vertical posts must now extend at least 30 feet above the crossbar.)

Birthdays: Donny Anderson, 1943; Jim Langer, 1948; Thurman Thomas, 1966

Trivia: Who tied his own playoff record when he made five field goals and accounted for all of his team's points in a 15-6 win over the Ravens in the 2006 Playoffs?

Trivia Answer: Adam Vinatieri, with the Colts

MAY

17

On This Date: On May 17, 1969, Cleveland, Baltimore and Pittsburgh agreed to join the AFL teams to form the American Football Conference of the NFL. The NFL also agreed on a playoff format that would include one "wild card" team per conference.

Birthdays: Earl Morrall, 1934; Norv Turner, 1952; Jim Nantz, 1959; Matt Cassel, 1982; Matt Ryan, 1985

Trivia: What is the only team in NFL history to play in both the AFC and NFC Championship Games?

Trivia Answer: Seattle Seahawks

MAY

On This Date: On May 18, 1963, Ernie Davis, the first African-American to win the Heisman Trophy, died of leukemia at the age of 23. Davis, the #1 pick of the 1962 NFL Draft, never played in a regular season game. His #45 is retired by the Browns.

Birthdays: Ray Donaldson, 1958; Will Wolford, 1964; Craig Hentrich, 1971; Flozell Adams, 1975; Olandis Gary, 1975; Vince Young, 1983; Robert Quinn, 1990

Trivia: What Browns Hall of Famer became the NFL's first black general manager with the Ravens in 2002?

Trivia Answer: Ozzie Newsome

MAY

On This Date: On May 19, 1935, the NFL adopted a collegiate draft, with the first to be held in 1936.

Birthdays: Archie Manning, 1949; London Fletcher, 1975; Marcedes Lewis, 1984; Brandon Carr, 1986

Trivia: What Eagles founder was instrumental in instituting the NFL Draft and later served as the league's commissioner?

Trivia Answer: Bert Bell

MAY

On This Date: On May 20, 2009, Michael Vick was released from prison after serving a year and a half sentence for his role in running a dogfighting ring. Vick would make his NFL return when he signed with the Philadelphia Eagles later in the year.

Birthdays: Bud Grant, 1927; Leroy Kelly, 1942; Rick Upchurch, 1952; Wendell Tyler, 1955; Tim Krumrie, 1960

Trivia: Before starring with the Eagles, what dynamic Villanova runner was the first player in college football history at any level to have 1,000 yards rushing and 1,000 receiving in the same season in 1998?

Trivia Answer: Brian Westbrook

MAY

On This Date: On May 21, 1962, the U.S. District Court ruled against the AFL in its antitrust suit against the NFL. The AFL had charged the NFL with conspiracy and having a monopoly in areas of expansion, television and player signings.

Birthdays: Ara Parseghian, 1923; Johnny Majors, 1935; Dave Wannstedt, 1952; Dorsey Levens, 1970; Ricky Williams, 1977; Eddie Royal, 1986; Devin Funchess, 1994

Trivia: "Bambi" was the first AFL star selected to the Pro Football Hall of Fame. Who is he?

Trivia Answer: Lance Alworth

MAY

On This Date: On May 22, 2001, the NFL changed its division alignment starting with the 2002 season. With the emergence of the Houston Texans, the league switched to a four-division format with four teams in each division in the two conferences.

Birthdays: Mick Tingelhoff, 1940; Dre Bly, 1977; Julian Edelman, 1986

Trivia: Which two NFL divisions are comprised solely of AFL franchises?

Trivia Answer: The AFC East and the AFC West

MAY

On This Date: On May 23, 2011, Peyton Manning underwent a surgical procedure for a bulging disc in his neck. The lingering injury would require more attention and ultimately force him to miss the entire 2011 season, effectively ending his time with the Colts.

Birthdays: Larry Garron, 1937; James Hasty, 1965; Jay Feely, 1976; Charles Rogers, 1981; Aaron Donald, 1991

Trivia: Before coaching a Super Bowl team in the 2000s, what quarterback led the Colts in passing yardage in each of the four seasons before Peyton Manning joined the NFL?

Trivia Answer: Jim Harbaugh

MAY

On This Date: On May 24, 2004, Maurice Clarett lost his legal suit against the NFL. Clarett was challenging the league's rule that a player must be three years removed from their high school graduation in order to be eligible for the draft. As a result, Clarett sat out a year, was drafted by the Denver Broncos in 2005 and released after an unimpressive training camp.

Birthdays: Jim Mora, 1935; Timmy Brown, 1937; Jason Babin, 1980; Nelson Agholor, 1993

Trivia: When the Bears signed this legend days after his final college game in 1925, it led the NFL to implement a rule saying a player couldn't be signed until his college's senior class graduated. Who is he?

Trivia Answer: Red Grange

MAY

On This Date: On May 25, 1999, the Washington Redskins were sold to D.C. businessman Daniel Snyder. Exactly six years later, NFL owners approved the purchase of another NFC team, the Minnesota Vikings, to real estate developer Zygi Wilf.

Birthdays: Cookie Gilchrist, 1935; Keith Hamilton, 1971; Tarik Glenn, 1976; Brian Urlacher, 1978; Shawne Merriman, 1984

Trivia: What New York Giants owner is the only person ever to win both an Oscar and a Super Bowl ring?

Trivia Answer: Steve Tisch

MAY

On This Date: On May 26, 1969, ABC signed a deal with the NFL to televise *Monday Night Football* starting with the 1970 season. *MNF* would become one of television's longest primetime running shows with Howard Cosell and an entertaining parade of others in the broadcast booth.

Birthdays: Brent Musburger, 1939; Dan Pastorini, 1949; Wesley Walker, 1955; Greg Lloyd, 1965

Trivia: Who replaced Mike Tirico as the play-by-play man for *Monday Night Football* for the 2016 season?

Trivia Answer: Sean McDonough

MAY

On This Date: On May 27, 1968, George Halas officially called it a career as the head coach of the Chicago Bears. Papa Bear won six titles during his 40-year tenure, all with the same franchise.

Birthdays: Walt Kiesling, 1903; Jackie Slater, 1954; Nick Lowery, 1956; Antonio Freeman, 1972; Danny Wuerffel, 1974; Darrell Russell, 1976; Nick Barnett, 1981; Darnell Dockett, 1981; Vontae Davis, 1988

Trivia: Before leading the Bears, Lovie Smith made his first trip to the Super Bowl in 2001 as the defensive coordinator for what team?

Trivia Answer: St. Louis Rams

MAY

On This Date: On May 28, 2006, beleaguered running back Ricky Williams signed with the Toronto Argonauts of the CFL. The signing occurred after Williams was suspended for the entire NFL season for failing his fourth drug test. He would return to the NFL the following year, and would have another 1,000-yard season with Miami in 2009.

Birthdays: Jim Thorpe, 1888; Eugene Robinson, 1963; Michael Oher, 1986; T.J. Yates, 1987; NaVorro Bowman, 1988; Percy Harvin, 1988

Trivia: Before starting his NFL career in 1999, Ricky Williams played minor league baseball in what team's farm system?

Trivia Answer: Philadelphia Phillies

MAY

On This Date: On May 29, 1987, Brett Favre graduated from Hancock North Central High School, where he played for his father, Irvin. Favre would begin his freshman year of college at Southern Miss as the seventh-string quarterback.

Birthdays: Matt Bryant, 1975; Shaun King, 1977; Ezekiel Ansah, 1989

Trivia: In 2003, the day after his father's death, Brett Favre put on an inspiring performance on *Monday Night Football* as the Packers blew out what team 41-7?

Trivia Answer: Oakland Raiders

MAY

On This Date: On May 30, 1943, Gale Sayers was born. The Kansas Comet was the most electrifying runner of his era, albeit a short one. Due to a knee injury, Sayers played only from 1965-71 with the Chicago Bears. Even so, he was inducted into the Pro Football Hall of Fame in 1977 and selected for the NFL's 75th Anniversary All-Time Team.

Birthdays: Bucko Kilroy, 1921; Gale Sayers, 1943; Lydell Mitchell, 1949; John Alt, 1962

Trivia: True or False? At 34, Gale Sayers was the youngest person ever inducted into the Pro Football Hall of Fame.

Trivia Answer: True

MAY

On This Date: On May 31, 1943, Joe Namath was born. The Hall of Fame quarterback was an AFL icon who will forever be remembered for his bold Super Bowl III guarantee in which his Jets won their only championship to date by upsetting the Baltimore Colts.

Birthdays: Joe Namath, 1943; Norm Johnson, 1960; Lorenzo Alexander, 1983; Jordy Nelson, 1985; Quincy Enunwa, 1992

Trivia: Who passed for more yards than anyone else in the history of the American Football League?

Trivia Answer: Jack Kemp (21,130 yards)

JUNE

On This Date: On June 1, 1994, the NFL launched NFL Sunday Ticket, a new satellite TV subscription that would allow viewers to watch every regular season game every Sunday.

Birthdays: Alan Ameche, 1933; Larry Centers, 1968; Santana Moss, 1979

Trivia: NBC broadcast the Super Bowl in both 1993 and '94. Those games marked the first time that the same teams met in a Super Bowl in back-to-back years. Who were they?

Trivia Answer: Dallas Cowboys and Buffalo Bills (SBs XXVII and XXVIII)

JUNE

On This Date: On June 2, 1992, Bill Parcells underwent open-heart surgery. It was the fourth heart-related procedure in less than a year for Parcells, who would be healthy enough to become the head coach of the New England Patriots in 1993.

Birthdays: Garo Yepremian, 1944; Lawrence McCutcheon, 1950; Jeff Siemon, 1950; Eddie Lacy, 1990

Trivia: What safety was involved in the injuries that ended seasons for both Tom Brady (2008) and Wes Welker (2009)?

Trivia Answer: Bernard Pollard

JUNE

On This Date: On June 3, 2013, David "Deacon" Jones died at the age of 74. Considered one of the best pass rushers football has ever seen, Jones actually coined the term "sack." With the Rams, he was the NFL's Defensive Player of the Year in 1967 and '68.

Birthdays: Emmitt Thomas, 1943; Sam Mills, 1959; Az-Zahir Hakim, 1977

Trivia: Who led the NFL in sacks as a Chief in 2007 (with 15.5) and later as a Viking in 2011 (with 22)?

Trivia Answer: Jared Allen

JUNE

On This Date: On June 4, 1990, Penn State was admitted as the 11th member of the Big Ten. The storied institution, which had been an Independent, would begin playing football games in their new conference in 1993.

Birthdays: Ed Newman, 1951; Jim Lachey, 1963; Jesse James, 1994

Trivia: Before he was the head coach of the Houston Texans, he held the same position at Penn State. Who is he?

Trivia Answer: Bill O'Brien

JUNE

On This Date: On June 5, 1984, the NFL held a supplemental draft for college seniors who had already signed with either the CFL or USFL. The number one pick was quarterback Steve Young, drafted by the Tampa Bay Buccaneers, while Reggie White went fourth to the Philadelphia Eagles.

Birthdays: Marion Motley, 1920; Art Donovan, 1925; Mike Zimmer, 1956; Kevin Faulk, 1976; Torry Holt, 1976; Marques Colston, 1983

Trivia: Deeming him a bust, the Buccaneers traded away Steve Young days before the 1987 NFL Draft and selected what player with the #1 overall pick?

Trivia Answer: Vinny Testaverde

JUNE

On This Date: On June 6, 2011, the Bowl Championship Series stripped the University of Southern California of its 2004 title, leaving the season without a BCS champion. The NCAA found that Reggie Bush had received improper benefits while at the school. Bush voluntarily forfeited his Heisman Trophy.

Birthdays: Bobby Mitchell, 1935; Dave Grayson, 1939; Rueben Mayes, 1963; Olindo Mare, 1973; DeAndre Hopkins, 1992

Trivia: With Seattle's Super Bowl XLVIII win, USC's Pete Carroll became the third man to win college and NFL titles, joining what two former Dallas Cowboys coaches?

Trivia Answer: Jimmy Johnson (Miami) and Barry Switzer (Oklahoma)

JUNE

On This Date: On June 7, 1986, the Kansas City Royals selected Bo Jackson in the fourth round of the MLB Draft. Less than two months earlier, the Tampa Bay Buccaneers made Jackson the #1 pick of the 1986 NFL Draft.

Birthdays: Goose Gonsoulin, 1938; Terance Mathis, 1967; Terrell Buckley, 1971; Christian McCaffrey, 1996

Trivia: What is Bo Jackson's given first name?

Trivia Answer: Vincent

JUNE

On This Date: On June 8, 1966, the battle between the AFL and NFL came to an end with the announcement of the merger of the leagues. While the first "Super Bowl" would take place at the end of the season, it would not be until 1970 that the two leagues became one.

Birthdays: Byron "Whizzer" White, 1917; Herb Adderley, 1939; Dave Jennings, 1952; Troy Vincent, 1971

Trivia: With three, what franchise won more American Football League championships than any other?

Trivia Answer: Dallas Texans/Kansas City Chiefs

JUNE

On This Date: On June 9, 1960, the AFL signed a multi-year television deal with ABC, becoming a legitimate threat to the NFL.

Birthdays: Tedy Bruschi, 1973; Olin Kreutz, 1977; Josh Cribbs, 1983

Trivia: After his playing days, what 1980s ABC show did Fran Tarkenton co-host with John Davidson and Cathy Lee Crosby?

Trivia Answer: That's Incredible!

JUNE

On This Date: On June 10, 1995, NFL quarterback Rodney Peete married actress Holly Robinson. Peete was in the middle of a 16-year career that would make stops in six different cities. The celebrity couple has four children together.

Birthdays: Larry Brooks, 1950; Dan Fouts, 1951; Marion Barber, 1983; Kyle Williams, 1983

Trivia: What *Married...with Children* star was a rookie linebacker in Pittsburgh's 1969 training camp before his successful television career?

Trivia Answer: Ed O'Neill

JUNE

On This Date: On June 11, 1903, 1913 and 1956, three significant figures in football history were born - Ernie Nevers, Vince Lombardi and Joe Montana. Nevers was a part of the inaugural 1963 Hall of Fame class. Lombardi would join him in Canton eight years later, and Montana in 2000.

Birthdays: Ernie Nevers, 1903; Vince Lombardi, 1913; Gary Fencik, 1954; Joe Montana, 1956; Brock Marion, 1970

Trivia: If football's Hall of Famers were listed alphabetically, who would come first?

Trivia Answer: Herb Adderley

JUNE

On This Date: On June 12, 2006, Ben Roethlisberger underwent seven hours of facial reconstruction surgery following an accident in which he rammed his motorcycle into a car that turned left in front of him. The Super Bowl-winning quarterback would make a full recovery.

Birthdays: Carlton Williamson, 1958; Dallas Clark, 1979; Larry Foote, 1980

Trivia: Slash ranks a distant third behind Terry Bradshaw and Ben Roethlisberger for touchdown passes as a Steeler. Who is he?

Trivia Answer: Kordell Stewart

JUNE

On This Date: On June 13, 2014, Hall of Fame football coach Chuck Noll died at the age of 82. Noll, once a player for the Cleveland Browns, was the head coach of the Pittsburgh Steelers for over 20 years. He guided the team to four Super Bowl titles in his time there.

Birthdays: Red Grange, 1903; Sam Adams, 1973; Ameer Abdullah, 1993

Trivia: Who had a higher winning percentage coaching the Steelers: Chuck Noll or Bill Cowher?

Trivia Answer: Cowher, .623 to .566

JUNE

On This Date: On June 14, 1994, the New York Giants released Phil Simms, effectively ending his NFL career. The release came as a surprise to the 38-year-old Simms, who had just had a Pro Bowl year in leading his team to an 11-5 playoff season.

Birthdays: Stew Barber, 1939; Tom Matte, 1939; Ben Davidson, 1940; Chris McAlister, 1977; Trai Turner, 1993; Sammy Watkins, 1993

Trivia: On what Showtime football program does Phil Simms currently appear?

Trivia Answer: Inside the NFL

JUNE

On This Date: On June 15, 1914, Knute Rockne graduated magna cum laude from the University of Notre Dame. Before he was named head coach of the Fighting Irish in 1918, Rockne taught chemistry.

Birthdays: Mike Holmgren, 1948; Derek Anderson, 1983; Jake Locker, 1988; Jay Ajayi, 1993

Trivia: Before he became a Packers Hall of Famer, who won the 1956 Heisman Trophy even though his Notre Dame squad went 2-8 that year?

Trivia Answer: Paul Hornung

JUNE

On This Date: On June 16, 1970, Bears running back Brian Piccolo died at 26 from embryonal cell carcinoma. The following year, *Brian's Song*, which recounted Piccolo's life and friendship with Gale Sayers, aired as a TV movie.

Birthdays: Al Cowlings, 1947; Luis Sharpe, 1960; Jerricho Cotchery, 1982; Josh Sitton, 1986; Jermaine Gresham, 1988

Trivia: *Invincible*, made in 2006, is a movie about what former Eagle?

Trivia Answer: Vince Papale

JUNE

On This Date: On June 17, 1994, the O.J. Simpson Bronco chase took over television. Game 5 of the NBA Finals between the Knicks and Rockets was supposed to be the sports news of the night. However, it was ultimately forced into a split-screen on NBC as coverage of the infamous car chase became a live TV event for the ages.

Birthdays: Elroy "Crazylegs" Hirsch, 1923; Bobby Bell, 1940; Dermontti Dawson, 1965; Jason Hanson, 1970; Kyle Boller, 1981; Albert Haynesworth, 1981; Justin Bethel, 1990; Amari Cooper, 1994

Trivia: In 1972, the Cowboys had their first 1,000-yard rusher. In 1994, his boy was the third pick in the NBA Draft. Name the father/son combo.

Trivia Answer: Calvin Hill and son Grant Hill

JUNE

On This Date: On June 18, 1963, Bruce Smith, one of the NFL defensive greats, was born. Synonymous with the word "sack," Smith is the all-time career leader with 200. The defensive end appeared in four Super Bowls with the Bills and was named to the NFL's All-Decade Teams of the '80s and '90s.

Birthdays: Romeo Crennel, 1947; Bruce Smith, 1963; Jeff Saturday, 1975; Antonio Gates, 1980; Chris Harris, 1989; Jason Verrett, 1991

Trivia: What Ravens rookie tied an NFL record in 2003 when he recorded a sack in each of his first four games as a pro?

Trivia Answer: Terrell Suggs

JUNE 19

On This Date: On June 19, 1943, because of a shortage of players due to World War II, the Philadelphia Eagles and the Pittsburgh Steelers were granted permission to merge for one season by the NFL. The team was known as the Steagles and divided home games between Philly and Pittsburgh.

Birthdays: Leo Nomellini, 1924; Charlie Cowan, 1938; Patrick Surtain, 1976; Peter Warrick, 1977; Rashard Mendenhall, 1987; Xavier Rhodes, 1990; C.J. Mosley, 1992

Trivia: The Eagles share their home stadium, Lincoln Financial Field, with which college football team?

Trivia Answer: Temple Owls

JUNE 20

On This Date: On June 20, 1935, Len Dawson was born. The Hall of Famer was the MVP in the Chiefs' lone Super Bowl win (IV) and led the AFL in passing touchdowns four times.

Birthdays: Len Dawson, 1935; LaVar Arrington, 1978; Darren Sproles, 1983; Matt Flynn, 1985; Terrelle Pryor, 1989; Leonard Williams, 1994

Trivia: Len Dawson's backup on Kansas City's Super Bowl IV title team became the first man to win a ring as a player and a head coach when his Raiders took Super Bowl XV. He is…?

Trivia Answer: Tom Flores

JUNE

21

On This Date: On June 21, 1963, Bob Hayes set
a world record when he ran the 100-yard dash in 9.1
seconds. The Florida A&M star would go on to have a
Hall of Fame career as a Cowboys receiver.

Birthdays: Bob Gain, 1929; Mike McCormack, 1930;
Wade Phillips, 1947; Al Wilson, 1977

Trivia: At the 2017 NFL Scouting Combine, who broke Chris
Johnson's record when he ran the 40-yard dash in 4.22 seconds?

Trivia Answer: John Ross

JUNE

22

On This Date: On June 22, 1997, the Barcelona
Dragons, led by MVP Jon Kitna, won World Bowl V over
the Rhein Fire. The World League of American Football (later
named NFL Europe) operated from 1991-2007.

Birthdays: Davey O'Brien, 1917; Bobby Douglass, 1947;
Eric Green, 1967; Kurt Warner, 1971; Champ Bailey, 1978

Trivia: Before he found a permanent home in Pittsburgh, what
future star was sent to play with NFL Europe's Rhein Fire after
being signed by the Bills in 2004?

Trivia Answer: James Harrison

JUNE

On This Date: On June 23, 1939, Bears Hall of Famer Bronko Nagurski defeated Lou Thesz to claim the National Wrestling Association world title.

Birthdays: Tony Hill, 1956; Robert Brooks, 1970; Brandon Stokley, 1976; Matt Light, 1978; LaDainian Tomlinson, 1979

Trivia: What WWE wrestler tried out for the Vikings in 2004 and was cut before the regular season?

Trivia Answer: Brock Lesnar

JUNE

On This Date: On June 24, 1922, the American Professional Football Association changed its name to the National Football League.

Birthdays: Shaun Ellis, 1977; Antoine Winfield, 1977; Kelechi Osemele, 1989

Trivia: Playing By The Rules: A field goal attempt grazes the helmet of the offensive right guard before it clears the uprights. Does the field goal count?

Trivia Answer: No

JUNE

On This Date: On June 25, 1992, 27-year-old Jerome Brown died in a car accident along with his 12-year-old nephew. The Eagles defensive lineman was coming off back-to-back Pro Bowl seasons. Brown's #99 would be retired by Philadelphia at the start of the upcoming season.

Birthdays: Phyllis George, 1949; Marcus Stroud, 1978; Matt Schaub, 1981; Kevin White, 1992

Trivia: In 2009, what Eagle became the first player to be selected to the Pro Bowl at two different positions in the same year?

Trivia Answer: DeSean Jackson, as a wide receiver and return specialist

JUNE

On This Date: On June 26, 1968, Shannon Sharpe was born. One of the best tight ends in NFL history, Sharpe played 12 of his 14 seasons with Denver and owns three Super Bowl rings, two with the Broncos and one with the Ravens. He joined the Hall of Fame in 2011.

Birthdays: Shannon Sharpe, 1968; Chad Clifton, 1976; Chad Pennington, 1976; Michael Vick, 1980

Trivia: In his 2011 induction speech, Shannon Sharpe claimed he was "the only pro football player that's in the Hall of Fame" who was "the second best player in my own family." Who was he referring to?

Trivia Answer: His brother, Sterling Sharpe

JUNE

On This Date: On June 27, 2009, Eagles wide receiver Hank Baskett wed Playboy Playmate Kendra Wilkinson. Baskett, whose NFL career came to an end in 2011, would join Wilkinson as a reality TV personality.

Birthdays: Doug Buffone, 1944; Julius Thomas, 1988; Bobby Wagner, 1990

Trivia: In 2012, NFL QB Christian Ponder tied the knot with what ESPN reporter?

Trivia Answer: Samantha Steele

JUNE

On This Date: On June 28, 2016, Buddy Ryan died at the age of 85. In his 35-year coaching career, Ryan was perhaps best known as the defensive guru behind the 1985 Bears title team. Sons Rex and Rob have both enjoyed success coaching at the NFL level.

Birthdays: Chuck Howley, 1936; Raymond Chester, 1948; John Elway, 1960; Jay Schroeder, 1961; Marvin Jones, 1972; Karim Abdul-Jabbar, 1974

Trivia: What team handed the 1985 Super Bowl champion Bears their lone loss of the NFL season?

Trivia Answer: Miami Dolphins, 38-24

JUNE

On This Date: On June 29, 1949, Dan Dierdorf was born. The 13-year Cardinals offensive tackle was born in Canton and enshrined in Canton as a member of the Hall of Fame. After his playing days, he would work for ABC's *Monday Night Football* and CBS as a color commentator.

Birthdays: Bill Brown, 1938; Claude Humphrey, 1944; Dan Dierdorf, 1949

Trivia: What sportscaster is the son of a former President and CEO of the Green Bay Packers?

Trivia Answer: Kevin Harlan (His dad is Bob Harlan.)

JUNE

On This Date: On June 30, 1984, the Los Angeles Express and Michigan Panthers of the USFL played a postseason contest that turned into the longest game in pro football history. The teams went into a third overtime before the Express won, 27-21, after 93 minutes and 33 seconds of playing time.

Birthdays: Bill Lenkaitis, 1946; Roy Green, 1957; Miles Austin, 1984

Trivia: In 1977, one of the most famous plays in NFL history transpired as the Raiders defeated the Colts in a classic double overtime playoff game. Who did Oakland QB Ken Stabler hit on a 42-yard "Ghost to the Post" play to keep his team alive?

Trivia Answer: Dave Casper

JULY

On This Date: On July 1, 1989, NFL owners voted to form the World League of American Football (later NFL Europe). The developmental league for NFL players would last 17 years.

Birthdays: Pat Donovan, 1953; Mike Haynes, 1953; Dave Waymer, 1958; Ryan Diem, 1979

Trivia: What longtime Cowboys boss was the commissioner of the World League of American Football in the early 1990s?

Trivia Answer: Tex Schramm

JULY

On This Date: On July 2, 2015, Lions Hall of Fame tight end Charlie Sanders died at the age of 68. Sanders made the Pro Bowl in each of his first four NFL seasons and is a member of the 1970s All-Decade Team.

Birthdays: Joe Pisarcik, 1952; Troy Brown, 1971; Carlos Rogers, 1981; BenJarvus Green-Ellis, 1985; Chad Henne, 1985

Trivia: The record for interceptions in one season was set in 1952 by what future Lions Hall of Famer?

Trivia Answer: Dick "Night Train" Lane, with 14 (then as a Ram)

JULY

On This Date: On July 3, 1968, the NFL Players
Association voted to strike over pension benefits. Owners
responded by locking players out during training camp.
The matter was resolved in less than two weeks, resulting in
the first NFL collective bargaining agreement.

Birthdays: Jethro Pugh, 1944; Elmo Wright, 1949;
Neil O'Donnell, 1966; Jordan Reed, 1990

Trivia: What is the score of a forfeited NFL game?

Trivia Answer: 2-0

JULY

On This Date: On July 4, 2003, former Chicago
Bears defensive tackle William "Refrigerator" Perry competed
in Nathan's annual Hot Dog Eating Contest. Refrigerator put
down just four hot dogs before dropping out. The winner,
Takeru Kobayashi, ate 44 dogs in 12 minutes, a world record at
the time.

Birthdays: Al Davis, 1929; Erich Barnes, 1935;
Floyd Little, 1942; Emerson Boozer, 1943; Bob Breunig, 1953;
La'Roi Glover, 1974; Josh McCown, 1979; Will Smith, 1981

Trivia: What Bear was the first football player ever to appear
on a box of Wheaties?

Trivia Answer: Red Grange

JULY

On This Date: On July 5, 1956, James Lofton was born. Lofton's Hall of Fame career spanned 16 years with five teams, mostly the Packers and Bills. The wide receiver was an eight-time Pro Bowler.

Birthdays: John McKay, 1923; Billy Howton, 1930; George Kunz, 1947; Johnny Rodgers, 1951; James Lofton, 1956; Richie Incognito, 1983; Malcolm Smith, 1989

Trivia: Before becoming a star in the broadcast booth, Cris Collinsworth was a Pro Bowl receiver for what NFL team during the 1980s?

Trivia Answer: Cincinnati Bengals

JULY

On This Date: On July 6, 2016, Russell Wilson married singer Ciara at the Peckforton Castle in Cheshire, England.

Birthdays: Fred Dryer, 1946; Joe Jacoby, 1959; Alvin Harper, 1968; Nnamdi Asomugha, 1981; Brandon Jacobs, 1982; Matt Kalil, 1989

Trivia: While he was in the broadcast booth for ABC, his wife performed the National Anthem at Super Bowl XXIX. Who are they?

Trivia Answer: Frank Gifford and Kathie Lee Gifford

JULY

On This Date: On July 7, 2005, wide receiver Tim Brown announced that he would sign a one-day contract with the Oakland Raiders and retire a Raider the next day. The wide receiver would be inducted into the Pro Football Hall of Fame in 2015.

Birthdays: Jerry Sherk, 1948; Michael McCrary, 1970; Darnay Scott, 1972; Michael Westbrook, 1972

Trivia: Tim Brown won the Heisman Trophy in 1987 while playing for what school?

Trivia Answer: Notre Dame

JULY

On This Date: On July 8, 1933, Art Rooney founded the Pittsburgh Steelers. One of the most storied franchises in football history, the Steelers have won more Super Bowls, six, than any other team.

Birthdays: Roone Arledge, 1931; John David Crow, 1935; Tommy Mason, 1939; Jack Lambert, 1952; Vic Beasley, 1992

Trivia: True or False? The Steelers are the only team to win back-to-back Super Bowls on more than one occasion.

Trivia Answer: True

JULY

On This Date: On July 9, 1932, a group of investors led by George Marshall bought an NFL franchise for the city of Boston. They contracted to play their home games at Braves Field, which was home of the National League baseball team. The football team, also named the Braves, would become the Redskins in 1933.

Birthdays: Clem Daniels, 1937; O.J. Simpson, 1947; Trent Green, 1970; Kelly Holcomb, 1973; Ben McAdoo, 1977

Trivia: Which has been airing longer on ESPN: *Sunday Night Baseball* or *Monday Night Football*?

Trivia Answer: Sunday Night Baseball, *which began in 1990 (MNF debuted in 1970, but did not come to ESPN until 2006.)*

JULY

On This Date: On July 10, 2003, Jon Bon Jovi was approved as an Arena Football League owner of the Philadelphia expansion franchise set to begin play in 2004. They would become known as the Soul.

Birthdays: Roger Craig, 1960; Darryl Talley, 1960; Urban Meyer, 1964; Antonio Brown, 1988; Cameron Jordan, 1989; Trent Richardson, 1990

Trivia: At Super Bowl XXVII in 1993, the success of what music legend's halftime show led to deliberate efforts to attract top performers for the event from then on?

Trivia Answer: Michael Jackson

JULY

On This Date: On July 11, 2000, Michael Irvin's retirement from the National Football League became official. The wide receiver would enter the Hall of Fame seven years later.

Birthdays: Len Hauss, 1942; Willie Anderson, 1975; Andre Johnson, 1981; Chris Cooley, 1982; Jacoby Jones, 1984; B.J. Raji, 1986; Patrick Peterson, 1990; Joey Bosa, 1995

Trivia: Michael Irvin played the part of Deacon Moss in the 2005 remake of what movie?

Trivia Answer: The Longest Yard

JULY

On This Date: On July 12, 1990, Commissioner Paul Tagliabue named NFL referee Jerry Seeman as the new NFL Director of Officiating. Seeman replaced Art McNally, who retired after 31 years working for the league. Mike Pereira would succeed Seeman in 2001.

Birthdays: Frank Ryan, 1936; Chad Brown, 1970; LeSean McCoy, 1988; Rodney Hudson 1989

Trivia: When you see a flag on the play, it's a yellow one. What color were NFL officials' flags until the mid-1960s?

Trivia Answer: White

JULY

On This Date: On July 13, 1972, Robert Irsay purchased the Los Angeles Rams. He then transferred ownership of the franchise to Carroll Rosenbloom in exchange for the Baltimore Colts.

Birthdays: Jack Kemp, 1935; Danny Abramowicz, 1945; Rod Marinelli, 1949; Mark Murphy, 1955; Tim Dwight, 1975; Jason Hatcher, 1982

Trivia: In 1980, the Giants and 49ers swapped defensive backs who would both later become NFL head coaches. New York sent Ray Rhodes to San Francisco in return for what 2000s Super Bowl winner?

Trivia Answer: Tony Dungy

JULY

On This Date: On July 14, 1985, the Baltimore Stars defeated the Oakland Invaders, 28-24, to win the final title of the United States Football League. The USFL would fold the following year.

Birthdays: Rosey Grier, 1932; Ken Willard, 1943; Ken Burrough, 1948; Monte Jackson, 1953; Darrelle Revis, 1985

Trivia: After his time as the head coach of the USFL's Stars, he would spend a decade in the same position with the New Orleans Saints. Who is he?

Trivia Answer: Jim Mora

JULY

15

On This Date: On July 15, 2003, Tex Schramm, the Hall of Fame team president and original GM of the Dallas Cowboys, died at the age of 83. Schramm was not only a pioneer, but also a football visionary and innovator from the formation of the Dallas Cowboys Cheerleaders to the implementation of instant replay.

Birthdays: Alex Karras, 1935; John Stallworth, 1952; Sammy Winder, 1959; Carnell Lake, 1967

Trivia: The reality television series *Dallas Cowboys Cheerleaders: Making the Team* airs each season on what cable television network?

Trivia Answer: CMT

JULY

16

On This Date: On July 16, 1992, Junious "Buck" Buchanan died at 51. Buchanan, a defensive lineman and AFL star with the Chiefs, had been diagnosed with lung cancer a week before his 1990 Hall of Fame induction.

Birthdays: Jimmy Johnson, 1943; Ron Yary, 1946; Gary Anderson, 1959; Barry Sanders, 1968; Aaron Glenn, 1972; Knowshon Moreno, 1987; Jordan Matthews, 1992

Trivia: What player, who spent the majority of his career with the Chiefs, was the first pure placekicker in the Pro Football Hall of Fame?

Trivia Answer: Jan Stenerud

JULY

On This Date: On July 17, 1990, Yankees outfielder Deion Sanders hit an inside-the-park home run after lining a shot past the outstretched glove of a fellow NFL star, Royals centerfielder Bo Jackson.

Birthdays: Daryle Lamonica, 1941; Scott Norwood, 1960; Eric Moulds, 1973; Kevin Curtis, 1978; Derrick Henry, 1994

Trivia: Colin Kaepernick was selected in the 43rd round of the 2009 Major League Baseball Draft by what team?

Trivia Answer: Chicago Cubs

JULY

On This Date: On July 18, 1969, Joe Namath agreed to sell his interest in Bachelors III, a New York nightclub, in order to resume his NFL career. Namath had retired the previous month after the league demanded he sell his share of the controversial hangout.

Birthdays: Jerome Barkum, 1950; Deion Branch, 1979; Jimmie Ward, 1991

Trivia: The younger brother of what NFL QB appeared on the 12th season of *The Bachelorette* in 2016?

Trivia Answer: Aaron Rodgers (His brother is Jordan Rodgers, also a quarterback, who had a brief stint in the NFL.)

JULY

On This Date: On July 19, 1994, cleaning tiles fell from the roof at Seattle's Kingdome, forcing the building to be closed until November. The Seahawks would play three of their regular season games at Husky Stadium on the University of Washington campus.

Birthdays: Jerry Smith, 1943; LeRoy Butler, 1968; Brent Grimes, 1983; Trent Williams, 1988

Trivia: Super Bowl XXX between the Steelers and Cowboys would be the last to be held on a college campus. Where was it?

Trivia Answer: Sun Devil Stadium, on the campus of Arizona State University

---

JULY

On This Date: On July 20, 1994, O.J. Simpson and his team of lawyers announced a $500,000 reward for any tips in the murder case of Nicole Brown Simpson and Ronald Goldman.

Birthdays: Dick Stanfel, 1927; Jake Scott, 1945; Jordan Gross, 1980; Troy Smith, 1984

Trivia: What 2007 event resulted in Bill Belichick being fined an NFL maximum of $500,000?

Trivia Answer: Spygate - The Patriots were found guilty of videoing an opponent's defensive signals.

JULY

On This Date: On July 21, 1994, Miami Dolphins owner Wayne Huizenga announced he had reached a new agreement with head coach Don Shula. Shula would become the Vice President/Head Coach and part owner of the franchise but would retire as head coach after the 1995 season.

Birthdays: Henry Ellard, 1961; David Carr, 1979; Jon Dorenbos, 1980; Kellen Winslow II, 1983; Taylor Lewan, 1991

Trivia: Who coached the Dolphins for a single season in 2007, in which Miami went 1-15?

Trivia Answer: Cam Cameron

JULY

On This Date: On July 22, 1995, the Los Angeles Raiders' move back to Oakland was approved. The Raiders had been in Los Angeles since 1982, when Al Davis moved the team there from Oakland after he could not get the city to expand the Oakland Coliseum.

Birthdays: Tim Brown, 1966; Keyshawn Johnson, 1972; Steven Jackson, 1983; Stevie Johnson, 1986; Sean Lee, 1986; Ezekiel Elliott, 1995

Trivia: The 49ers Levi's Stadium is actually located nearly 40 miles from San Francisco in what California city?

Trivia Answer: Santa Clara

JULY

On This Date: On July 23, 2012, the NCAA imposed harsh sanctions on Penn State following investigations into the Jerry Sandusky scandal. The school was hit with a $60 million fine, a four-year ban from postseason play and a cut in the number of football scholarships it could award.

Birthdays: Walt Garrison, 1944; Mark Jackson, 1963; Terry Glenn, 1974; Matt Birk, 1976; K.J. Wright, 1989

Trivia: Who recently became the only Penn State head coach besides Joe Paterno to lead the football team to a double-digit win season?

Trivia Answer: James Franklin, in 2016

JULY

On This Date: On July 24, 2003, the Denver Broncos waived Terrell Davis after he failed a physical due to his degenerative knees. Davis, the MVP of Super Bowl XXXII and a 2017 Hall of Famer, would retire at the age of 31 in August 2004 after a failed comeback attempt.

Birthdays: Willie Davis, 1934; Steve Grogan, 1953; Brian Blades, 1965; Blaine Bishop, 1970; Kevin Hardy, 1973; Mewelde Moore, 1982; Donte Whitner, 1985; Maurkice & Mike Pouncey, 1989

Trivia: Who signed with the Browns to become the highest-paid center in NFL history in 2006 before having to retire due to a serious knee injury?

Trivia Answer: LeCharles Bentley

JULY

On This Date: On July 25, 2004, running back Ricky Williams shocked the Miami Dolphins and the entire NFL when he announced he was planning to retire from the league at the age of 27. He would return to the team in 2005.

Birthdays: Walter Payton, 1954; Gerard Warren, 1978; Corey Graham, 1985

Trivia: What NFL team has retired the #12 in honor of their fans, "The 12th Man"?

Trivia Answer: Seattle Seahawks

JULY

On This Date: On July 26, 1939, Bob Lilly was born. Called "the greatest defensive tackle in NFL history" by *The Sporting News* and named to the All-Century NFL Team, Lilly played for the Dallas Cowboys from 1961 to 1974. He became a Hall of Famer in 1980.

Birthdays: Bob Waterfield, 1920; Tommy McDonald, 1934; Bob Lilly, 1939; Robert Gallery, 1980

Trivia: True or False? In 1961, Bob Lilly was the very first draft pick in Dallas Cowboys history.

Trivia Answer: True

JULY

On This Date: On July 27, 1929, Charles O'Brien sold the Chicago Cardinals to David Jones for $25,000. The team would eventually be owned by the Bidwill family and become the St. Louis Cardinals who would become the Phoenix Cardinals who would become the Arizona Cardinals (in 1994).

Birthdays: Haven Moses, 1946; Reggie McKenzie, 1950; Hugh Green, 1959; Antoine Bethea, 1984; Ryan Tannehill, 1988

Trivia: Because fictional receiver Rod Tidwell wore this wideout's #85 Cardinals jersey, footage of what NFL player appeared in the hit movie *Jerry Maguire*?

Trivia Answer: Rob Moore

JULY

On This Date: On July 28, 1999, Barry Sanders retired at the age of 31. Just 1,500 yards shy of breaking Walter Payton's all-time rushing record, Sanders said he had lost his passion for the game and stepped away from football.

Birthdays: Dexter Jackson, 1977; Chris Samuels, 1977; Julian Peterson, 1978; DeMeco Ryans, 1984

Trivia: At Oklahoma State, Barry Sanders played in the same backfield with what fellow future Hall of Fame runner?

Trivia Answer: Thurman Thomas

JULY

On This Date: On July 29, 1986, a jury in a New York U.S. District Court awarded the United States Football League $1 in its $1.7 billion antitrust suit against the NFL. Because damages in antitrust cases are tripled, the USFL actually received $3.

Birthdays: Pepper Johnson, 1964; Jonathan Cyprien, 1990; Dak Prescott, 1993

Trivia: In 2000, what former Cowboy won the Texas state lottery and took home $28 million?

Trivia Answer: Thomas "Hollywood" Henderson

JULY

On This Date: On July 30, 1971, the Baltimore Colts beat the College All-Stars, 24-17, in the Chicago All-Star Game. The game traditionally pitted the NFL's last champion versus the best college players, but since it was the NFL team's first preseason game, the Colts decided to go with their rookies against the college all-stars.

Birthdays: Jim Mandich, 1948; Dwight White, 1949; Reggie Roby, 1961; Robert Porcher, 1969

Trivia: In 1954, the Baltimore Colts achieved an NFL first that had nothing to do with their play on the field. What was it?

Trivia Answer: They formed the NFL's first official cheerleading team.

JULY

On This Date: On July 31, 1971, the NFL inducted its newest Hall of Fame class, including a few historic figures - Jim Brown, Vince Lombardi and Y.A. Tittle.

Birthdays: Norm Snead, 1939; Gerry Philbin, 1941; Chris Hinton, 1961; Kevin Greene, 1962; Gus Frerotte, 1971; Jason Gildon, 1972; Chris Weinke, 1972; Jonathan Ogden, 1974; Marty Booker, 1976; Tim Couch, 1977; DeMarcus Ware, 1982; Brian Orakpo, 1986; A.J. Green, 1988

Trivia: Of Cowboys Hall of Fame trio Troy Aikman, Michael Irvin and Emmitt Smith, which one did not attend school in Florida?

Trivia Answer: Aikman, who played at Oklahoma and UCLA (Irivn attended Miami and Smith, Florida.)

AUGUST

On This Date: On August 1, 2001, Minnesota Vikings offensive lineman Korey Stringer died from complications due to heat stroke suffered during a training camp practice.

Birthdays: Cliff Branch, 1948; Greg Bell, 1962; Marion Butts, 1966; Edgerrin James, 1978; Mike Wallace, 1986

Trivia: Tackle Matt Kalil made the Pro Bowl as a rookie in 2012 with the Vikings. He joined his brother Ryan, a fellow offensive lineman, on what squad in 2017?

Trivia Answer: Carolina Panthers

AUGUST

On This Date: On August 2, 1967, the New Orleans Saints played their first-ever NFL contest, a 16-7 exhibition loss to the L.A. Rams. After a 5-1 preseason, the Saints finished their inaugural regular season at 3-11.

Birthdays: Lamar Hunt, 1932; Matt Hazeltine, 1933; Billy Cannon, 1937; Tom Rafferty, 1954; Brandon Browner, 1984; Golden Tate, 1988; Laremy Tunsil, 1994

Trivia: True or False? New Orleans was awarded the Saints NFL franchise on November 1, 1966, on "All Saints Day."

Trivia Answer: True

AUGUST

On This Date: On August 3, 1986, the NFL redefined the word "football" in England. More than 80,000 people jammed London's Wembley Stadium for the first "American Bowl" to watch an exhibition game between the defending champion Chicago Bears and the Dallas Cowboys. The Bears won, 17-6.

Birthdays: Marv Levy, 1925; Maxie Baughan, 1938; Lance Alworth, 1940; Todd Christensen, 1956; Trevor Pryce, 1975; Tom Brady, 1977; Kris Jenkins, 1979; Tyrod Taylor, 1989; Dante Fowler, Jr., 1994; Todd Gurley, 1994

Trivia: While he has a Nigerian first name, this 2000s Giants sack artist was born in London. Who is he?

Trivia Answer: Osi (Ositadimma) Umenyiora

AUGUST

On This Date: On August 4, 1986, the USFL announced it was suspending its operations for one year, but not folding. They never played another game.

Birthdays: John Riggins, 1949; Bob Baumhower, 1955; Clyde Simmons, 1964

Trivia: What one-time Bears head coach is the only man to ever coach teams in the NFL, college football, the USFL, World Football League and CFL?

Trivia Answer: Jack Pardee

AUGUST

On This Date: On August 5, 1967, Emlen Tunnell became the first African-American to be inducted into the Pro Football Hall of Fame. The defensive back played a decade with the New York Giants and finished his career up in Green Bay.

Birthdays: Roman Gabriel, 1940; Bruce Coslet, 1946; William Roberts, 1962; C.J. Spiller, 1987

Trivia: The Giants retired the #1 in 1935, the first uniform number retired in pro sports history, for this man, a Hall of Fame coach who is credited with introducing the screen pass. Who?

Trivia Answer: Ray Flaherty

AUGUST

On This Date: On August 6, 1983, the NFL
played its first game in Europe. The Minnesota Vikings
beat the St. Louis Cardinals by a score of 28-10 at Wembley
Stadium in a preseason clash in London, England.

Birthdays: Ken Riley, 1947; Charlie Whitehurst, 1982;
Donte Moncrief, 1993

Trivia: As a teenager, what future Cardinals star was a ball boy
for the Minnesota Vikings?

Trivia Answer: Larry Fitzgerald

AUGUST

On This Date: On August 7, 2005, MVP
quarterbacks Dan Marino and Steve Young were
inducted into the Hall of Fame. They were joined by
Fritz Pollard and Benny Friedman.

Birthdays: John Gilliam, 1945; Alan Page, 1945;
Tim McGee, 1964; Shane Lechler, 1976; Jordan Cameron, 1988;
Tashaun Gipson, 1990

Trivia: Peyton Manning has won more NFL MVPs than
anyone. How many?

Trivia Answer: Five

AUGUST

On This Date: On August 8, 2006, Roger Goodell was unanimously selected by the owners to replace Paul Tagliabue as Commissioner of the NFL. Goodell had previously been the league's Chief Operating Officer.

Birthdays: Fred Miller, 1940; Brian Sipe, 1949; Bruce Matthews, 1961; Jim Sweeney, 1962; Pierre Garcon, 1986

Trivia: Playing By The Rules: A defensive player bats a forward pass up in the air. The quarterback catches his own pass. May he throw another forward pass?

Trivia Answer: No

AUGUST

On This Date: On August 9, 2015, Hall of Fame player and sportscaster Frank Gifford died a week shy of his 85th birthday. After 12 seasons and eight Pro Bowls with the New York Giants, Gifford spent 27 years in the *Monday Night Football* broadcast booth.

Birthdays: Gene Lipscomb, 1931; Bill Forester, 1932; Jim Kiick, 1946; Henry Marshall, 1954; Doug Williams, 1955; Louis Lipps, 1962; Kevin Mack, 1962; Chris Miller, 1965; Deion Sanders, 1967; Adewale Ogunleye, 1977; Matt Moore, 1984; JaMarcus Russell, 1985

Trivia: Howard Cosell delivered what tragic news to a *Monday Night Football* audience that was tuned in to watch a 1980 Dolphins vs. Patriots game?

Trivia Answer: The death of John Lennon

AUGUST

On This Date: On August 10, 2002, the Seattle Seahawks' stadium, currently known as CenturyLink Field, opened with a Seahawks loss to the Indianapolis Colts, 28-10, in a preseason contest.

Birthdays: Eddie Meador, 1937; Walt Harris, 1974; Samari Rolle, 1976; Matt Prater, 1984

Trivia: Marshawn Lynch's 67-yard touchdown run against the Saints in the 2010 NFL Playoffs that registered a small tremor at the stadium was later given what nickname?

Trivia Answer: The Beast Quake

AUGUST

On This Date: On August 11, 1919, the Green Bay Packers were born. The football club, named after its sponsor, the Indian Packing Company, was founded by George Calhoun and Curly Lambeau.

Birthdays: Bill Munson, 1941; Otis Taylor, 1942; Andy Lee, 1982; Tracy Porter, 1986

Trivia: Between 1939-62, the Packers won four titles, all coming from victories over what NFL franchise?

Trivia Answer: New York Giants

AUGUST

On This Date: On August 12, 1978, the career of promising Patriots receiver Darryl Stingley came to an abrupt end when he was paralyzed after a hit in a preseason game from Oakland's Jack Tatum. Stingley would die in 2007 due to complications from quadriplegia.

Birthdays: R.C. Thielemann, 1955; Plaxico Burress, 1977; Derrick Burgess, 1978; Chris Chambers, 1978; Delanie Walker, 1984

Trivia: With New England, Randy Moss broke Jerry Rice's single-season receiving touchdown mark in 2007 by finishing the year with how many scores?

Trivia Answer: 23

AUGUST

On This Date: On August 13, 2016, the NFL returned to Los Angeles as the Rams hosted the Dallas Cowboys in an exhibition contest. Over 89,000 turned out at the L.A. Memorial Coliseum to see the Rams win, 28-24. The contest was also the first at the pro level for Dak Prescott, who impressed with two TD passes in defeat.

Birthdays: Chris Hanburger, 1941; Cris Dishman, 1965; William Thomas, 1968; Elvis Grbac, 1970; Devin & Jason McCourty, 1987

Trivia: The L.A. Memorial Coliseum has been the longtime home of what historic college football franchise?

Trivia Answer: USC Trojans

AUGUST 14

On This Date: On August 14, 1959, Lamar Hunt announced his intentions to start a rival football league to the NFL. At a meeting in Chicago, representatives from six different cities set plans to begin play in 1960.

Birthdays: Wellington Mara, 1916; John Brodie, 1935; Neal Anderson, 1964; Adam Timmerman, 1971; Wayne Chrebet, 1973; Greg Ellis, 1975; Michael Pittman, 1975; Mike Vrabel, 1975; Roy Williams, 1980; Julius Jones, 1981; Tim Tebow, 1987; Kiko Alonso, 1990

Trivia: Gale Sayers opted to sign with the Bears after what AFL team also drafted him in 1965?

Trivia Answer: Kansas City Chiefs

AUGUST 15

On This Date: On August 15, 1994, an all-time NFL record for attendance was set in Mexico City. A crowd of 112,376 gathered to watch the Houston Oilers defeat the Dallas Cowboys, 6-0, in a preseason game.

Birthdays: Lionel Taylor, 1935; Gene Upshaw, 1945; Sam Cunningham, 1950; Gary Kubiak, 1961; Bubby Brister, 1962; Yancey Thigpen, 1969

Trivia: After it was determined they had been using pre-recorded crowd noise during home games, the NFL stripped what team of their fifth round draft pick in 2016?

Trivia Answer: Atlanta Falcons

AUGUST

On This Date: On August 16, 1965, Miami was awarded an AFL franchise. Lawyer Joseph Robbie and actor Danny Thomas paid $7.5 million for the team and named it the Dolphins after a committee searched through 19,843 entries.

Birthdays: Amos Alonzo Stagg, 1862; Frank Gifford, 1930; Christian Okoye, 1961; Ben Coates, 1969; Kevin Williams, 1980; Ryan Kerrigan, 1988; A.J. Bouye, 1991

Trivia: When asked about the Dolphins defense prior to Super Bowl VI, Cowboys coach Tom Landry said he couldn't recall any specific players. This inspired what Miami moniker?

Trivia Answer: The No-Name Defense

AUGUST

On This Date: On August 17, 2002, the New England Patriots' stadium, currently known as Gillette Stadium, opened with a 16-15 Patriots victory over the Eagles in a preseason contest.

Birthdays: Isiah Robertson, 1949; Jon Gruden, 1963; John Offerdahl, 1964; Ed McCaffrey, 1968; Antwaan Randle El, 1979

Trivia: The Patriots played in what venue for 30 years, from 1971-2001?

Trivia Answer: Foxboro Stadium (originally Schaefer Stadium and later Sullivan Stadium)

AUGUST

On This Date: On August 18, 2009, Brett Favre made his final NFL stop, signing on with the Minnesota Vikings. Favre would post career numbers as he led his new team all the way to the NFC title game vs. the Saints. He would have a less-successful 2010 before finally calling it quits for good.

Birthdays: Matt Snell, 1941; Greg Pruitt, 1951; Brian Mitchell, 1968; Adalius Thomas, 1977; Bart Scott, 1980; Jeremy Shockey, 1980; Dontari Poe, 1990

Trivia: Brett Favre's very first pass as a Packer was one to remember. What happened?

Trivia Answer: He caught his own deflected pass for a -7 yard play.

AUGUST

On This Date: On August 19, 1997, Microsoft co-founder Paul Allen purchased the Seattle Seahawks from Ken Behring for $200 million.

Birthdays: Anthony Munoz, 1958; Morten Andersen, 1960; Bobby Hebert, 1960; David Patten, 1974; David Boston, 1978; Thomas Jones, 1978; Nate Burleson, 1981; Jermon Bushrod, 1984; Kirk Cousins, 1988

Trivia: The Seattle Seahawks became a franchise in 1974 after Lloyd W. Nordstrom signed on the dotted line. Why wasn't the owner present for the team's very first NFL game?

Trivia Answer: Nordstrom died months before the 1976 season began. His family retained the team's ownership.

AUGUST

On This Date: On August 20, 1920, the American Professional Football Conference was formed. The league was created in order to give structure to professional football and consisted of four Ohio teams - the Akron Pros, Canton Bulldogs, Cleveland Indians and Dayton Triangles.

Birthdays: Dave Kocourek, 1937; Gary Collins, 1940; Oronde Gadsden, 1971; Mitch Trubisky, 1994

Trivia: The Decatur Staleys began play in 1920. They are still in existence, currently known under what name?

Trivia Answer: Chicago Bears

AUGUST

On This Date: On August 21, 1999, Cleveland Browns Stadium, the home of the "new" Browns, opened as the Vikings beat Cleveland by a score of 24-17 in a preseason game. The venue would become known as FirstEnergy Stadium in 2013.

Birthdays: Pete Retzlaff, 1931; Joe Morrison, 1937; Willie Lanier, 1945; Archie Griffin, 1954; Mickey Shuler, 1956; Gary Hogeboom, 1958; Jim McMahon, 1959; Mike Evans, 1993

Trivia: The Browns had back-to-back #1 picks in 1999 and 2000. Who did they take the year after selecting Tim Couch?

Trivia Answer: Courtney Brown

AUGUST

On This Date: On August 22, 1909 and 1941, two Giants Hall of Famers were born – Mel Hein and Bill Parcells. Hein played 15 seasons for New York and is the only offensive lineman to be named league MVP. Parcells guided Big Blue to their first two Super Bowl titles.

Birthdays: Mel Hein, 1909; Paul Maguire, 1938; Bill Parcells, 1941; Wes Chandler, 1956; Jahri Evans, 1983; Mohamed Sanu, 1989; Randall Cobb, 1990

Trivia: What former Giants Pro Bowl guard is married to the daughter of former coach Tom Coughlin?

Trivia Answer: Chris Snee, who married Kate Coughlin

AUGUST

On This Date: On August 23, 1985, a Louisville court awarded Packers legend Paul Hornung $1.16 million from the NCAA, who had banned him as a college football analyst for betting on games.

Birthdays: Sonny Jurgensen, 1934; Rayfield Wright, 1945; Mark Ingram, 1965; Cortez Kennedy, 1968; Hugh Douglas, 1971; Rex Grossman, 1980

Trivia: Dimetrios Georgios Synodinos is the real name of what late NFL oddsmaker?

Trivia Answer: Jimmy "The Greek" Snyder

AUGUST

On This Date: On August 24, 1984, the USFL decided to directly compete with the NFL with the announcement that they would move their season from spring to fall starting in 1986.

Birthdays: Mike Shanahan, 1952; Arian Foster, 1986; Allen Robinson, 1993

Trivia: Tommy Maddox was the one and only MVP of what league that folded in 2001 after a single spring season?

Trivia Answer: XFL

AUGUST

On This Date: On August 25, 1988, Art Rooney, the founding owner of the Pittsburgh Steelers, died at 87. Rooney was an idolized Steel City figure who, after 41 seasons of ownership, finally brought home a championship in 1975 as the Steelers defeated the Vikings in Super Bowl IX.

Birthdays: Charlie Sanders, 1946; Doug English, 1953; Cornelius Bennett, 1965; Marvin Harrison, 1972

Trivia: In Super Bowl IX, the game's MVP ran for more yards than the entire Minnesota offense produced. Who was it?

Trivia Answer: Franco Harris

AUGUST

On This Date: On August 26, 1996, the Tampa Bay Storm defeated the Iowa Barnstormers, 42-38, in Arena Bowl X. Future NFL head coach Jay Gruden quarterbacked the Storm, while future NFL MVP Kurt Warner was behind center for Iowa.

Birthdays: Donnie Shell, 1952; Barret Robbins, 1973; Drew Bennett, 1978

Trivia: While still playing in the NFL, what former Seahawks receiver was an owner of the Columbus Destroyers of the Arena Football League in the early 2000s?

Trivia Answer: Joey Galloway

AUGUST

On This Date: On August 27, 1960, the Dallas Cowboys registered their first NFL win, albeit a preseason one, against the New York Giants by the score of 14-3. The year proved to be a rather rude welcome to the NFL for the Cowboys as they went winless during the regular season (0-11-1).

Birthdays: Frank Leahy, 1908; Mack Brown, 1951; Michael Dean Perry, 1965; Rob Burnett, 1967; Ladell Betts, 1979; Rashean Mathis, 1980; Darren McFadden, 1987

Trivia: Before becoming the Cowboys head coach in 1960, Tom Landry was the defensive coordinator and Vince Lombardi the offensive coordinator for what NFL team?

Trivia Answer: New York Giants

AUGUST

On This Date: On August 28, 1955, the NFL played its first-ever overtime game, a preseason contest in which the Los Angeles Rams beat the New York Giants, 23-17, at Multnomah Stadium in Portland, Oregon. Before the game, promoter Harry Glickman asked for the league's okay to have overtime in case of a tie. Permission was granted and it laid the foundation for the overtime rule to finally be approved in 1974.

Birthdays: Jim Lynch, 1945; Bob Avellini, 1953; Nate Washington, 1983

Trivia: At 96 yards, what 49er provided the longest overtime rushing touchdown in NFL history in 1998 to send his team to victory over the Jets in their season opener?

Trivia Answer: Garrison Hearst

AUGUST

On This Date: On August 29, 2013, the NFL agreed to pay $765 million to settle lawsuits from over 4,000 former players who claimed they developed concussion-related health issues as a result of the on-field violence.

Birthdays: Carl Banks, 1962; Jamal Lewis, 1979; Jay Ratliff, 1981; Leon Washington, 1982

Trivia: What 49er would retire in 2015, one season after entering the NFL, citing concern over the many head injuries in the sport?

Trivia Answer: Chris Borland

AUGUST

On This Date: On August 30, 2003, New Mexico placekicker Katie Hnida became the first female player to score in a Division I-A game. She kicked two extra points in a 72-8 win over Texas State-San Marcos.

Birthdays: Coy Bacon, 1942; Marvin Powell, 1955; Shaun Alexander, 1977; Joe Staley, 1984; Duane Brown, 1985; Deone Bucannon, 1992

Trivia: At the University of New Mexico, what future NFL star linebacker scored several touchdowns as both a kick returner and receiver?

Trivia Answer: Brian Urlacher

AUGUST

On This Date: On August 31, 1997, Eddie George ran for 216 yards and scored a touchdown in the Oilers' first game in Tennessee. They beat the Oakland Raiders, 24-21, at the Liberty Bowl in Memphis.

Birthdays: Jim Finks, 1927; Tom Coughlin, 1946; Gary Johnson, 1952; Larry Fitzgerald, 1983

Trivia: What running back from the University of Tennessee went from an undrafted free agent in 2009 to the NFL's leading rusher in 2010?

Trivia Answer: Arian Foster

SEPTEMBER

On This Date: On September 1, 2007, the Appalachian State Mountaineers stunned the college football world with a 34-32 season opening win over the Michigan Wolverines. As a result of the shocking upset, Michigan dropped all the way from #5 to out of the AP Top 25 Poll.

Birthdays: Ray Flaherty, 1903; Bo Schembechler, 1929; George Saimes, 1941; Karl Mecklenburg, 1960; Hardy Nickerson, 1965; Zach Thomas, 1973; Jason Taylor, 1974; Aaron Schobel, 1977; Clinton Portis, 1981; Calais Campbell, 1986

Trivia: Michigan shut out Stanford, 49-0, in the inaugural edition of what Bowl Game way back in 1902?

Trivia Answer: Rose Bowl (then called the East-West Game)

SEPTEMBER

On This Date: On September 2, 1989, Southern Methodist University played in its first game since having the "death penalty" imposed on them for violating NCAA rules two years earlier. They lost 35-6 to Rice, a team that had lost its previous 18 games. It would take nearly two decades before they beat a ranked team.

Birthdays: Terry Bradshaw, 1948; Eric Dickerson, 1960; Tommy Maddox, 1971; Brian Westbrook, 1979

Trivia: Running backs Craig James and Eric Dickerson teamed up at SMU to form a backfield that went by what nickname?

Trivia Answer: The Pony Express

SEPTEMBER

On This Date: On September 3, 1970, the football world lost one of its most legendary figures when Vince Lombardi died at 57 years old. Lombardi, who won five championships in a seven-year period with the Packers, never had a losing season coaching in the NFL.

Birthdays: Ernest Givins, 1964; Bennie Blades, 1966; Renaldo Wynn, 1974; Jevon Kearse, 1976; Casey Hampton, 1977

Trivia: Vince Lombardi coached his last game with the Packers in 1968. What was the result?

Trivia Answer: A 33-14 win over the Oakland Raiders in Super Bowl II

SEPTEMBER

On This Date: On September 4, 1993, Penn State, playing in its first Big Ten game, beat Minnesota, 38-20, at Beaver Stadium, to win the inaugural Governor's Victory Bell. Nittany Lions' quarterback John Sacca and wide receiver Bobby Engram hooked up for four touchdowns in the victory.

Birthdays: Jason Fisk, 1972; Terence Newman, 1978; Hank Baskett, 1982

Trivia: What college football team's stadium is known as "The Big House"?

Trivia Answer: Michigan

SEPTEMBER

On This Date: On September 5, 2013, Denver's Peyton Manning tied an NFL record when he threw seven touchdown passes in a 49-27 season-opening win. The Broncos offense would go on to set regular season records for points scored and touchdowns.

Birthdays: Don Chandler, 1934; Billy Kilmer, 1939; Willie Gault, 1960; Tony Martin, 1965; Brad Hopkins, 1970; Leonard Davis, 1978; Colt McCoy, 1986

Trivia: In addition to Peyton Manning, what other NFL quarterback threw seven touchdown passes in a single game in 2013?

Trivia Answer: Nick Foles, with the Eagles

SEPTEMBER

On This Date: On September 6, 1980, in his first college game, Herschel Walker led Georgia back from a 15-point deficit against Tennessee, rushing for 84 yards and two scores in the Bulldogs' 16-15 win in Knoxville. Georgia would go on to win the national title that year.

Birthdays: Brendon Ayanbadejo, 1976; Ryan Clady, 1986; Ryan Shazier, 1992

Trivia: In the 1995 Peach Bowl, what future Steeler completed 31 of 59 passes for 413 yards as a sophomore quarterback for the University of Georgia?

Trivia Answer: Hines Ward

SEPTEMBER

On This Date: On September 7, 1963, the Pro Football Hall of Fame officially opened in Canton, Ohio. The first class inducted included Sammy Baugh, Red Grange, George Halas, Don Hutson, Curly Lambeau, Bronko Nagurski and Jim Thorpe.

Birthdays: Paul Brown, 1908; Forrest Blue, 1945; John Brockington, 1948; Bert Jones, 1951; Bruce Armstrong, 1965; Erik Williams, 1968

Trivia: While his only season with them was the final one of his career, Franco Harris became the first player from what team to be inducted into the Pro Football Hall of Fame in 1990?

Trivia Answer: Seattle Seahawks

SEPTEMBER

On This Date: On September 8, 2002, the Houston Texans became just the second NFL team to win their expansion debut (the 1961 Vikings were the first), surprising the Dallas Cowboys, 19-10, at Reliant Stadium. Rookie QB David Carr threw two touchdown passes in the victory.

Birthdays: Lem Barney, 1945; L.C. Greenwood, 1946; Amani Toomer, 1974; Malcom Floyd, 1981; Terrance Williams, 1989; Matt Barkley, 1990; Tyler Eifert, 1990

Trivia: Dom Capers, the first head coach of the Texans, was also the first head coach of what expansion team during the 1990s?

Trivia Answer: Carolina Panthers

SEPTEMBER

On This Date: On September 9, 1960, the Denver Broncos defeated the Boston Patriots, 13-10, in the first ever AFL game.

Birthdays: Dick LeBeau, 1937; Johnny Robinson, 1938; Ron McDole, 1939; Joe Theismann, 1949; Bob Stoops, 1960; Jack Trudeau, 1962; Matthew Slater, 1985

Trivia: What linebacker and original Patriot became the first President of the AFL Players Association in the mid-1960s?

Trivia Answer: Tom Addison

SEPTEMBER

On This Date: On September 10, 1989, Deion Sanders returned a punt 68 yards for a touchdown in his NFL debut with the Atlanta Falcons. Five days earlier, Sanders hit a home run as a New York Yankee. "Prime Time" remains the only athlete to play in both a Super Bowl (with the Cowboys and 49ers) and World Series (with the Braves).

Birthdays: Buck Buchanan, 1940; Charlie Waters, 1948; Gary Danielson, 1951; Kimble Anders, 1966; Sammy Knight, 1975; Desmond Trufant, 1990

Trivia: What 1960s Packer who also played baseball with the Senators is the only other man besides Deion Sanders to have played in an MLB game and a Super Bowl?

Trivia Answer: Tom Brown

SEPTEMBER

On This Date: On September 11, 2011, Carolina's Cam Newton became the first rookie to throw for over 400 yards in his NFL debut, a 28-21 loss to the Cardinals. The NFL's #1 pick passed for 422 yards and two touchdowns.

Birthdays: Paul "Bear" Bryant, 1913; Tom Landry, 1924; Don Mosebar, 1961; Dan Quinn, 1970; Mack Strong, 1971; Ed Reed, 1978

Trivia: In 2008, who became the first-ever coach/QB combo to win their NFL debut together?

Trivia Answer: John Harbaugh and Joe Flacco, with the Ravens

SEPTEMBER

On This Date: On September 12, 2004, with a 20-16 win at Chicago, the Detroit Lions snapped the longest road losing streak in NFL history at 24 games.

Birthdays: Ralph Neely, 1943; John "Frenchy" Fuqua, 1946; Deron Cherry, 1959; Ki-Jana Carter, 1973; Dan Koppen, 1979; Nick Hardwick, 1981; Andrew Luck, 1989

Trivia: The Lions have won only one postseason contest since their 1957 NFL championship victory. Who did they defeat in the 1991 Playoffs?

Trivia Answer: Dallas Cowboys

SEPTEMBER

On This Date: On September 13, 2015, Marcus
Mariota became the first quarterback to record a perfect 158.3
rating in his first NFL game. Mariota threw for four touchdowns,
all in the first half, completing 13 of 15 passes for 209 yards. The
Titans routed Jameis Winston and the Buccaneers, 42-14.

Birthdays: Mike Pagel, 1960; Brad Johnson, 1968;
Davone Bess, 1985; A.J. McCarron, 1990; Zach Zenner, 1991

Trivia: Against Seattle in 1986, what Jet became the first player
in NFL history to throw for over 400 yards in a game and earn a
perfect quarterback rating of 158.3?

Trivia Answer: Ken O'Brien

SEPTEMBER

On This Date: On September 14, 2003, Baltimore
Ravens' running back Jamal Lewis set the single-game rushing
record when he ran for 295 yards and two scores on 30 carries
in a 33-13 victory over Cleveland. Adrian Peterson would top
Lewis' mark by a single yard in 2007.

Birthdays: Michael Crabtree, 1987; Ronnie Hillman, 1991;
Chance Warmack, 1991; Deshaun Watson, 1995

Trivia: In 2009, his fourth season in Cleveland, he ran for 286
yards and three touchdowns in a game against the Chiefs. Before
that, he hadn't even surpassed 250 in an entire season. Who is
he?

Trivia Answer: Jerome Harrison

SEPTEMBER

On This Date: On September 15, 2002, Raiders quarterback Rich Gannon began his record-tying streak of six consecutive games with 300 or more passing yards when he threw for 403 against the Steelers in a 30-17 victory. Gannon finished the year with a record ten 300-yard games.

Birthdays: Merlin Olsen, 1940; Pete Carroll, 1951; LeRoy Irvin, 1957; Joe Morris, 1960; Dan Marino, 1961; Earnest Byner, 1962; Will Shields, 1971; David Diehl, 1980; Marshal Yanda, 1984

Trivia: Rich Gannon, a fourth round pick of the Patriots in 1987, was traded to what team after he balked at the idea of switching from quarterback to running back?

Trivia Answer: Minnesota Vikings

SEPTEMBER

On This Date: On September 16, 1989, Raghib "Rocket" Ismail returned two kickoffs for TDs as No. 2-ranked Notre Dame defeated the No. 1-ranked Michigan Wolverines, 24-19, at Ann Arbor, Michigan.

Birthdays: Bob DeMarco, 1938; Larry Grantham, 1938; Wilbert Montgomery, 1954; Chester McGlockton, 1969

Trivia: What Auburn Tiger's 2013 "Kick Six" took down 11-0 Alabama and instantly became a top moment in college football history?

Trivia Answer: Chris Davis (He returned a 57-yard missed field goal for a touchdown, giving Auburn a 34-28 win over Alabama.)

SEPTEMBER

On This Date: On September 17, 1961, the
Minnesota Vikings played their first NFL game,
defeating the Chicago Bears, 37-13. Also debuting that
day was Fran Tarkenton, who threw four touchdown passes
in his very first NFL start.

Birthdays: George Blanda, 1927; Anthony Carter, 1960;
Mark Brunell, 1970

Trivia: In the 2012 postseason, what Viking became the first
quarterback in NFL history to start a playoff game after not
having thrown one pass during that year's regular season?

Trivia Answer: Joe Webb

SEPTEMBER

On This Date: On September 18, 2014, Atlanta's
Devin Hester returned a punt 62 yards for a score to set an NFL
record with his 20th career return for a touchdown. Hester
topped Deion Sanders' mark as the Falcons routed Tampa Bay,
56-14.

Birthdays: Darryl Stingley, 1951; Billy Sims, 1955;
Jeff Bostic, 1958; Chip Banks, 1959; Dashon Goldson, 1984

Trivia: What player set an NFL record in 2003 when he
returned a kickoff or punt for a touchdown in four consecutive
games?

Trivia Answer: Dante Hall

SEPTEMBER 19

On This Date: On September 19, 2004, Jerry Rice failed to catch a pass in a Raiders win over the Bills. Rice had gone 274 straight games with a reception in a streak that dated back to December of 1985.

Birthdays: Charlie Conerly, 1921; Abner Haynes, 1937; Larry Brown, 1947; Nat Moore, 1951; Dan Hampton, 1957; Brett Keisel, 1978; Kenny Britt, 1988; Stephon Gilmore, 1990

Trivia: In 2015, who set a new NFL record with his sixth 100-catch season while also breaking the Jets single-season record for catches?

Trivia Answer: Brandon Marshall

SEPTEMBER 20

On This Date: On September 20, 1987, Walter Payton broke Jim Brown's NFL record for rushing touchdowns with his 107th in a victory over Tampa Bay. Payton ended his career with 110, though his mark has since been surpassed.

Birthdays: Jim Taylor, 1935; Butch Byrd, 1941; Tommy Nobis, 1943; Matt Blair, 1950; Eric Turner, 1968; Dante Hall, 1978; T.J. Lang, 1987; Coby Fleener, 1988; Carlos Hyde, 1991

Trivia: At what small school did Walter Payton play his college ball?

Trivia Answer: Jackson State

SEPTEMBER

On This Date: On September 21, 1970, the
Cleveland Browns defeated the New York Jets, 31-21,
in the first-ever *Monday Night Football* broadcast.

Birthdays: Jon Kitna, 1972; Mike Anderson, 1973;
Kevin Carter, 1973; Jeff Backus, 1977; Greg Jennings, 1983;
Reggie Nelson, 1983; Dwayne Bowe, 1984; Jimmy Clausen, 1987;
Doug Baldwin, 1988

Trivia: In a 2009 *Monday Night Football* game, the Colts came
out on top despite having the ball for just 14 minutes and 53
seconds. Who did they defeat, 27-23?

Trivia Answer: Miami Dolphins

SEPTEMBER

On This Date: On September 22, 1991, Don
Shula, the NFL's all-time winningest head coach, won
his 300th game. The Dolphins defeated the Packers, 16-13,
for the landmark victory.

Birthdays: Harold Carmichael, 1949; Chester Taylor, 1979;
Gary Barnidge, 1985; Denard Robinson, 1990

Trivia: Who has the most wins of any NFL head coach that has
never won a Super Bowl?

Trivia Answer: Marty Schottenheimer

SEPTEMBER

23

On This Date: On September 23, 2007, for the first time in NFL history, two players had 200+ yards receiving in the same game. Philadelphia's Kevin Curtis had 11 catches for 221 yards, while Detroit's Roy Williams caught nine balls for 204 yards. The Eagles routed the Lions, 56-21.

Birthdays: Bob Vogel, 1941; Marty Schottenheimer, 1943; Tunch Ilkin, 1957; Marvin Lewis, 1958; John Harbaugh, 1962; Tony Mandarich, 1966; Bryant McKinnie, 1979; Chris Johnson, 1985

Trivia: In 2005, who became the first undrafted player in NFL history to hit the 10,000-yard receiving mark?

Trivia Answer: Rod Smith

SEPTEMBER

24

On This Date: On September 24, 1994, Kordell Stewart's 64-yard Hail Mary pass to Michael Westbrook gave Colorado a stunning 27-26 last-second win over Michigan.

Birthdays: John Mackey, 1941; "Mean" Joe Greene, 1946; Terry Metcalf, 1951; Joe Washington, 1953; Eddie George, 1973; Kabeer Gbaja-Biamila, 1977; Vontaze Burfict, 1990

Trivia: What unknown receiver did Aaron Rodgers hit for a 41-yard Hail Mary score to ultimately send Green Bay's 2015 postseason contest with Arizona into overtime?

Trivia Answer: Jeff Janis (The Packers would lose in OT.)

SEPTEMBER

On This Date: On September 25, 2006, the Saints played their first game in New Orleans since Hurricane Katrina devastated the city the previous year. A Steve Gleason blocked punt that was returned for a score by Curtis Deloatch marked one of the most dramatic moments in team history. New Orleans defeated Atlanta, 23-3.

Birthdays: John Lynch, 1971; Matt Hasselbeck, 1975; Aldon Smith, 1989; Brandin Cooks, 1993

Trivia: What member of the Super Bowl XXXV champion Ravens was later diagnosed with ALS and became a source of inspiration for Baltimore's Super Bowl XLVII title?

Trivia Answer: O.J. Brigance

SEPTEMBER

On This Date: On September 26, 1965, Baltimore running back Lenny Moore failed to score a touchdown vs. Green Bay, ending his record streak of 18 straight games with a TD. LaDainian Tomlinson would match Moore's mark in 2005.

Birthdays: Dave Casper, 1951; Henry Lawrence, 1951; Wes Hopkins, 1961; Craig Heyward, 1966; Larry Izzo, 1974; T.J. Houshmandzadeh, 1977; D'Qwell Jackson, 1983

Trivia: In 2002, what runner set an NFL record by scoring five first half touchdowns in a game between the Seahawks and Vikings?

Trivia Answer: Shaun Alexander

SEPTEMBER

On This Date: On September 27, 1975, Kansas' Nolan Cromwell ran for 294 yards, an NCAA record for a quarterback, in a 20-0 shutout over Oregon State. Cromwell, normally a safety for the Jayhawks, was making his first start as a QB.

Birthdays: Rob Moore, 1968; Alonzo Spellman, 1971; Dion Lewis, 1990

Trivia: Richard Sherman was named a Freshman All-American at Stanford, but not at cornerback. What position did he play at the beginning of his college career?

Trivia Answer: Wide receiver

SEPTEMBER

On This Date: On September 28, 1951, Rams quarterback Norm Van Brocklin set a record that still stands when he threw for 554 yards in a single game, defeating the New York Yanks. Exactly 18 years later, Minnesota QB Joe Kapp picked apart Baltimore for 449 yards and a record-tying seven TD passes to defeat the Colts.

Birthdays: Tom Harmon, 1919; Charley Taylor, 1941; Mel Gray, 1948; Steve Largent, 1954; Irving Fryar, 1962; David Fulcher, 1964; Jake Reed, 1967; Tyler Lockett, 1992

Trivia: In 1943, what Bears Hall of Famer threw for over 400 yards and seven TD passes in a single game, becoming the first NFL player to accomplish either feat?

Trivia Answer: Sid Luckman

SEPTEMBER 29

On This Date: On September 29, 2002, Jerry Rice surpassed Walter Payton's NFL career record of 21,264 yards from scrimmage as his Raiders defeated the Titans. Rice would finish his career with 23,540.

Birthdays: Bum Phillips, 1923; Jimmy Patton, 1933; Dave Wilcox, 1942; Ken Norton Jr., 1966; Ray Buchanan, 1971; Chris Hope, 1980; Calvin Johnson, 1985

Trivia: When Jerry Rice joined the Seahawks in 2004, Steve Largent agreed to "unretire" his jersey number, as it was the same as the NFL's all-time leading receiver. What was it?

Trivia Answer: 80

SEPTEMBER 30

On This Date: On September 30, 1973, in his final NFL season, San Diego Chargers quarterback Johnny Unitas became the first player to surpass 40,000 yards passing when he hit Mike Garrett for a 30-yard completion against Cincinnati. Unitas would call it a career after the season.

Birthdays: Wayne Walker, 1936; Brentson Buckner, 1971; Jamal Anderson, 1972; Justin Smith, 1979; Adam "Pac-Man" Jones, 1983; David Bakhtiari, 1991

Trivia: True or False? Johnny Unitas never threw for 4,000 yards in a single season.

Trivia Answer: True

OCTOBER

On This Date: On October 1, 1989, defensive
end Ed "Too Tall" Jones recorded the 1,000th tackle of his
career, a bright note in an otherwise dismal year for the
Dallas Cowboys, who went 1-15 in Jimmy Johnson's first
season as head coach.

Birthdays: Conrad Dobler, 1950; Rudi Johnson, 1979;
Clive Walford, 1991

Trivia: In 1985, what 49er became the first player in NFL
history to gain 1,000 yards both rushing and receiving in the
same season?

Trivia Answer: Roger Craig (Marshall Faulk has since joined him.)

OCTOBER

On This Date: On October 2, 1994, Don and
Dave Shula became the first father and son in professional
sports history to coach against each other. Dave's Cincinnati
Bengals fell, 23-7, to Don's Dolphins.

Birthdays: Gary Green, 1955; Chuck Pagano, 1960;
Mark Rypien, 1962; Marcus Robertson, 1969; T.J. Yeldon, 1993

Trivia: Dick Nolan and his son, Mike, have each served as the
head coach of what NFL team?

Trivia Answer: San Francisco 49ers

OCTOBER

On This Date: On October 3, 1920, the Dayton Triangles beat the Columbus Panhandles 14-0 and the Rock Island Independents destroyed the Muncie Flyers 45-0 in the first ever games between NFL (then the American Pro Football Association) teams.

Birthdays: Jack Gregory, 1944; Bruce Arians, 1952; Anquan Boldin, 1980

Trivia: The "Flying Elvis" logo is featured on the helmet of what NFL team?

Trivia Answer: Patriots

OCTOBER

On This Date: On October 4, 2014, Jared Goff threw for 527 yards and five touchdowns as California beat Washington State in a 60-59 thriller. In defeat, WSU quarterback Connor Halliday set a new NCAA passing record with 734 yards and six touchdowns.

Birthdays: Billy Wade, 1930; Sam Huff, 1934; Jimmy Orr, 1935; Jabrill Peppers, 1995

Trivia: Three years before he became a Wisconsin Badger, as a freshman quarterback, Russell Wilson was the ACC Rookie of the Year for what school?

Trivia Answer: North Carolina State

OCTOBER

On This Date: On October 5, 2008, the Colts pulled off a stunning win after trailing the Texans by 17 with less than five minutes remaining. Six years later to the day, the Browns overcame a 28-3 deficit in Tennessee to complete the largest comeback victory by a road team in NFL history.

Birthdays: Barry Switzer, 1937; Drew Hill, 1956; Trace Armstrong, 1965; Dennis Byrd, 1966; Chad Lewis, 1971; Jesse Palmer, 1978; Trent Cole, 1982; Michael Roos, 1982; Travis Kelce, 1989

Trivia: In 1984, Maryland stunned Miami and all of college football by coming back from 31-0 to win, 42-40. The man who would lead the biggest comeback in NFL history was under center for the Terps that day. Who?

Trivia Answer: Frank Reich (He quarterbacked the Bills in the 1992 postseason.)

OCTOBER

On This Date: On October 6, 1986, in a Seahawks win over the Chargers, Seattle's Steve Largent caught a pass in his 128th straight game, breaking Harold Carmichael's NFL mark. Meanwhile, San Diego's Charlie Joiner passed Don Maynard to become the NFL's all-time receiving yardage leader. (Jerry Rice now holds both of those records.)

Birthdays: Les Richter, 1930; Tony Dungy, 1955; Albert Lewis, 1960; J.J. Stokes, 1972; Richard Seymour, 1979

Trivia: In 2002, what receiver broke Herman Moore's single-season NFL record of 123 receptions?

Trivia Answer: Marvin Harrison (He ended the season with 143.)

OCTOBER

On This Date: On October 7, 1984, Walter Payton became the NFL's all-time leading rusher with 154 yards in a Bears 20-7 win over New Orleans. Payton's performance gave him 12,400 career rushing yards, breaking the record held by Jim Brown. (Emmitt Smith currently owns the career rushing record with 18,355 yards.)

Birthdays: Dick Jauron, 1950; Blair Thomas, 1967; Johnnie Morton, 1971; Priest Holmes, 1973; Charles Woodson, 1976; Jairus Byrd, 1986; Russell Okung, 1987; Olivier Vernon, 1990

Trivia: True or False? In his very first NFL game, Walter Payton surpassed 200 yards rushing.

Trivia Answer: False - He carried the ball eight times for a total of zero yards.

OCTOBER

On This Date: On October 8, 1988, Columbia University defeated Princeton, 16-13, ending the longest losing streak in Division I-AA college football history. The Lions streak of 44 straight losses began in 1983, a year after Northwestern ended their losing streak at 34, the previous record.

Birthdays: Tony Eason, 1959; Donnie Abraham, 1973; Rashaan Salaam, 1974; Ryan Pickett, 1979

Trivia: What team was on the wrong side of NFL history when it became the first to lose a playoff game to a club with a losing record, the 7-9 Seahawks, in 2011?

Trivia Answer: New Orleans Saints

OCTOBER

On This Date: On October 9, 1989, Art Shell, first black NFL head coach of the modern era, won his first game when the Raiders defeated the Jets, 14-7.

Birthdays: Mike Singletary, 1958; Jimbo Fisher, 1965; Roman Oben, 1972; Daryl Washington, 1986

Trivia: Art Shell was elected to the Pro Football Hall of Fame in 1989 for his standout Raiders career as a player at what position?

Trivia Answer: Offensive tackle

OCTOBER

On This Date: On October 10, 1981, future College and Pro Football Hall of Fame running back Marcus Allen rushed for 211 yards for USC in a 13-10 loss to Arizona at the L.A. Memorial Coliseum. It was Allen's fifth straight game in which he rushed for at least 200 yards, setting an NCAA record.

Birthdays: Bill Thompson, 1946; Brett Perriman, 1965; Brett Favre, 1969; Paul Posluszny, 1984; Ryan Mathews, 1987; Linval Joseph, 1988; Geno Smith, 1990

Trivia: What College Football Hall of Famer and Chiefs running back would return to his alma mater to become the Athletic Director for USC?

Trivia Answer: Mike Garrett

OCTOBER

On This Date: On October 11, 1981, the Rams' LeRoy Irvin returned six punts for a record 207 yards in a 37-35 win over Atlanta. Two of Irvin's punt returns were for touchdowns, 75 and 84 yards.

Birthdays: Joe Nash, 1960; Steve Young, 1961; Chris Spielman, 1965; Bobby Humphrey, 1966; Terrell Suggs, 1982

Trivia: In 1997, what Charger became the first NFL player to score touchdowns on an interception return, fumble return and kickoff return in the same season?

Trivia Answer: Rodney Harrison

OCTOBER

On This Date: On October 12, 1986, Walter Payton became the first player in NFL history to go over 20,000 all-purpose yards. He ran for 76 and gained 30 receiving yards in a 20-7 Bears victory over the Oilers.

Birthdays: Chris Chandler, 1965; Leon Lett, 1968; Charlie Ward, 1970; Ryan Clark, 1979; Adrian Wilson, 1979

Trivia: Walter Payton's son Jarrett was college teammates with Kellen Winslow, Jr., another son of a Hall of Famer, at what school?

Trivia Answer: University of Miami

OCTOBER

On This Date: On October 13, 1962, Jerry Rice was born. Rice, considered by many as the greatest football player of all-time, holds nearly every receiving record in the book.

Birthdays: Jerry Jones, 1942; Rich Kotite, 1942; Jerry Rice, 1962; Brian Dawkins, 1973; Quincy Carter, 1977; Brian Hoyer, 1985

Trivia: What 49er made "The Catch", the winning score that beat the Cowboys in the 1981 NFC title game and sent the 49ers to the Super Bowl?

Trivia Answer: Dwight Clark

OCTOBER

On This Date: On October 14, 1990, Houston quarterback Warren Moon threw for 369 yards and five TDs in a victory over the Bengals to become the first person to throw for over 20,000 yards in two different leagues (Moon passed for 21,228 yards in the CFL).

Birthdays: Jerry Glanville, 1941; Lance Rentzel, 1943; Charlie Joiner, 1947; Bob Kuechenberg, 1947; Keith Byars, 1963; Frank Wycheck, 1971; Javon Walker, 1978; Brandon Weeden, 1983; LaRon Landry, 1984; Justin Forsett, 1985; Jared Goff, 1994

Trivia: What trophy is given to the champion of the Canadian Football League?

Trivia Answer: Grey Cup

OCTOBER

On This Date: On October 15, 2005, USC kept its undefeated season going by defeating Notre Dame, 34-31. In a controversial ending, Reggie Bush appeared to illegally push Matt Leinart across the goal line for the winning score. The Trojans would lose their lone game of the season to Texas in the Rose Bowl.

Birthdays: Joe Klecko, 1953; Connor Barwin, 1986; Blaine Gabbert, 1989

Trivia: In 2016, Reggie Bush became the first running back in NFL history to carry the ball at least 10 times and have negative yardage on the season. What team was he playing for?

Trivia Answer: Buffalo Bills

OCTOBER

On This Date: On October 16, 1999, #4 Virginia Tech and Michael Vick embarrassed #16 Syracuse, 62-0. It was the worst shutout loss by a ranked team in the history of the Associated Press poll.

Birthdays: Walt Michaels, 1929; Rich Caster, 1948; Chris Doleman, 1961; Adrian Murrell, 1970; Kordell Stewart, 1972; Jermaine Lewis, 1974

Trivia: What Syracuse and later Colts pass rushing stud once took down Virginia Tech's Michael Vick 4.5 times in a single college game?

Trivia Answer: Dwight Freeney

OCTOBER

On This Date: On October 17, 1983, the Green
Bay Packers defeated the Washington Redskins, 48-47, in
the highest scoring game in *Monday Night Football* history.
The two teams combined for over 1,000 yards of total offense.

Birthdays: Ron Johnson, 1947; Steve McMichael, 1957;
Willie Snead, 1992

Trivia: In 2010, the Eagles set a *Monday Night* record for points
in a game. Who did they beat in a 59-28 shootout?

Trivia Answer: Washington Redskins

OCTOBER

On This Date: On October 18, 1924, Red Grange
put on one of the greatest shows in the history of college football
when his Illinois squad defeated Michigan, 39-14. After running
back the opening kick 95 yards for a touchdown, he scored on
runs of 67, 56 and 44 yards – all in the first quarter. He added
two TDs later in the game, accounting for 402 yards in all.

Birthdays: Keith Jackson, 1928; Forrest Gregg, 1933;
Boyd Dowler, 1937; Mike Ditka, 1939; Frank Beamer, 1946;
Bob Whitfield, 1971

Trivia: Three all-time great Bears figures attended the
University of Illinois. One is Red Grange. Who are the other two
Hall of Famers?

Trivia Answer: Dick Butkus and George Halas

OCTOBER

On This Date: On October 19, 2014, Peyton Manning threw his 509th career touchdown pass in a Broncos win over the 49ers when he connected with Demaryius Thomas. Manning, who broke Brett Favre's record, would finish his career with 539 TD passes.

Birthdays: Jim Mitchell, 1947; Lynn Dickey, 1949; Webster Slaughter, 1964; Leonard Little, 1974

Trivia: Of all the NFL quarterbacks whose last names begin with the letter Z, who has thrown the most touchdown passes?

Trivia Answer: Jim Zorn, 111

OCTOBER

On This Date: On October 20, 1963, Jim Brown surpassed the NFL career-rushing total of 8,378 yards set by Joe Perry. Brown ran for 144 yards on the day in the victory over the Eagles. He would up his total to 12,312 before retiring after the 1965 season.

Birthdays: Roosevelt Brown, 1932; Isaac Curtis, 1950; Ray Rhodes, 1950; Lee Roy Selmon, 1954; Dave Krieg, 1958; Ray Childress, 1962; Herman Moore, 1969; Dexter Coakley, 1972; Jamie Collins, 1989; Jeremy Hill, 1992

Trivia: Jim Brown starred in what 1967 war film that was based on a novel of the same name?

Trivia Answer: The Dirty Dozen

OCTOBER

On This Date: On October 21, 1973, Rams defensive end Fred Dryer became the first and only player to record two safeties in one game as the Rams defeated the Packers. Exactly 34 years later, Titans kicker Rob Bironas became the first NFL player to make eight field goals in one game. That included the game-winner to defeat the Texans, 38-36.

Birthdays: Mo Lewis, 1969; Joey Harrington, 1978; Willis McGahee, 1981; Antonio Smith, 1981

Trivia: The last time this scoring outcome occurred in the NFL was way back in 1943 when the Giants played the Lions. What was the result?

Trivia Answer: The game ended in a 0-0 tie.

OCTOBER

On This Date: On October 22, 1939, NBC became the first network to televise a professional football game. Barely 13,000 were on hand at Brooklyn's Ebbets Field as the Philadelphia Eagles lost to the Brooklyn Dodgers, 23-14.

Birthdays: Pete Pihos, 1923; Leonard Marshall, 1961; Hue Jackson, 1965; Heath Miller, 1982; Muhammad Wilkerson, 1989

Trivia: True or False? The New York Giants football team got their name from the city's MLB franchise.

Trivia Answer: True

OCTOBER

On This Date: On October 23, 2000, the New York Jets came back from a 30-7 fourth quarter deficit to stun the Miami Dolphins in a "Monday Night Miracle." The Jets scored 30 points in the fourth to send the game into overtime, ultimately prevailing 40-37.

Birthdays: John Heisman, 1869; Frank "Bruiser" Kinard, 1914; Winston Hill, 1941; Doug Flutie, 1962; Mike Tomczak, 1962; Bill O'Brien, 1969; Zach Brown, 1989

Trivia: In a 2005 "Monday Night Massacre," the Eagles were destroyed, 42-0, by what team?

Trivia Answer: Seattle Seahawks

OCTOBER

On This Date: On October 24, 2004, the Kansas City Chiefs made history when running backs Priest Holmes and Derrick Blaylock each rushed for four touchdowns in a 56-10 rout over the Falcons. Exactly six years later, DeAngelo Hall tied an NFL record with four interceptions as his Redskins beat the Bears.

Birthdays: Y.A. Tittle, 1926; Jay Novacek, 1962; Pat Williams, 1972; Corey Dillon, 1974; Chris Hogan, 1988; Jalen Ramsey, 1994

Trivia: Thanks to that 2004 game in which the Chiefs scored eight rushing TDs, who became the first offensive lineman ever named the AFC Offensive Player of the Week?

Trivia Answer: Brian Waters

OCTOBER

On This Date: On October 25, 1964, Jim Marshall provided an NFL blooper-reel fixture when he recovered a fumble and ran 66 yards the wrong way into his own end zone for a safety. Fortunately for Marshall, his Vikings hung on to defeat the 49ers.

Birthdays: Jack Kent Cooke, 1912; David Woodley, 1958; Pat Swilling, 1964; Chris Conley, 1992

Trivia: Playing By The Rules: If a blocked punt goes out of the kicking team's end zone, is it ruled a safety?

Trivia Answer: Yes

OCTOBER

On This Date: On October 26, 1929, Albie Booth, a 5'6", 144-pound sophomore tailback, entered the game with Yale trailing Army 13-0. Booth led Yale back from the deficit by running for two touchdowns and returning a punt for a score. He also kicked three extra points, accounting for his team's entire total in a shocking 21-13 upset over unbeaten Army.

Birthdays: Sid Gillman, 1911; Ed Brown, 1928; Chuck Foreman, 1950; Tom Condon, 1952; Bob Golic, 1957; Mike Pritchard, 1969; Jessie Armstead, 1970; Antonio Pierce, 1978

Trivia: In 2006, the (then) all-time leading scorer for the Packers accounted for all 16 Vikings points vs. the Panthers by kicking three field goals and throwing a 16-yard touchdown pass. Who is he?

Trivia Answer: Ryan Longwell

OCTOBER

On This Date: On October 27, 2013, Calvin Johnson set a record for the most receiving yards in a non-overtime game, 329, as his Lions beat the Cowboys in a 31-30 thriller. Megatron's mark came 11 years to the day after Dallas' Emmitt Smith passed Walter Payton as the all-time leading rusher in NFL history.

Birthdays: Bill George, 1929; John Kasay, 1969; Peerless Price, 1976; Brady Quinn, 1984; Bilal Powell, 1988

Trivia: What receiver finished the 2015 season as just the second NFL player to record back-to-back 1,600-yard seasons (after Calvin Johnson)?

Trivia Answer: Antonio Brown

OCTOBER

On This Date: On October 28, 1962, Giants Hall of Famer Y.A. Tittle threw for 505 yards and tied an NFL record with seven touchdown passes in a win over Washington.

Birthdays: Jim Katcavage, 1934; Mark Carrier, 1965; Steve Atwater, 1966; Terrell Davis, 1972; Calvin Pace, 1980

Trivia: What quarterback set the NFL record for consecutive completed passes, with 25, in 2015?

Trivia Answer: Miami's Ryan Tannehill

OCTOBER

On This Date: On October 29, 1995, Jerry Rice surpassed James Lofton to become the NFL's all-time leading receiver. Rice caught eight passes for 108 yards in a loss to the Saints to boost his total to 14,040. The legacy was far from complete, however, as Rice would end his career with an astounding 22,895 yards receiving.

Birthdays: Andy Russell, 1941; J.T. Smith, 1955; Charlie Brown, 1958; Michael Carter, 1960; Drew Rosenhaus, 1966; Travis Henry, 1978; Maurice Clarett, 1983; Andy Dalton, 1987; Janoris Jenkins, 1988

Trivia: At what small school did Jerry Rice break numerous NCAA Division I-AA records?

Trivia Answer: Mississippi Valley State

OCTOBER

On This Date: On October 30, 1971, Cornell running back Ed Marinaro became college football's Division I all-time leading rusher when he ran for 272 yards in a win over Columbia. Marinaro would finish his career with 4,715 yards and become the first person to surpass the 4,000-yard mark.

Birthdays: Dick Vermeil, 1936; Jim LeClair, 1950; Ty Detmer, 1967; Keith Brooking, 1975; Marcus Mariota, 1993

Trivia: Off the field, Ed Marinaro would become known for his role in what 1980s NBC police drama?

Trivia Answer: Hill Street Blues

OCTOBER

On This Date: On October 31, 1959, Oklahoma suffered its first and only conference defeat of the decade, losing to underdog Nebraska, 25-21.

Birthdays: Cal Hubbard, 1900; Brian Piccolo, 1943; Nick Saban, 1951; Bill Fralic, 1962; Lee Woodall, 1969

Trivia: Set from 2008-09, what team holds the record for the longest NFL regular season winning streak, at 23 games?

Trivia Answer: Indianapolis Colts

NOVEMBER

On This Date: On November 1, 1964, Cleveland's Jim Brown ran for 149 yards against Pittsburgh to become the first NFL player to reach 10,000 career rushing yards. Meanwhile, in the AFL, Houston's George Blanda was taking the high road- through the air - attempting 68 passes (a record that would stand for 30 yards) against Buffalo and completing 37 of them.

Birthdays: Tom Mack, 1943; Ted Hendricks, 1947; Kent Graham, 1968; Steve Hutchinson, 1977; Evan Mathis, 1981; Bruce Irvin, 1987; Robert Alford, 1988

Trivia: In 1989, what Colt became the fastest player ever to reach 10,000 yards rushing?

Trivia Answer: Eric Dickerson

NOVEMBER

On This Date: On November 2, 2014, Ben Roethlisberger became the first NFL quarterback to throw six touchdown passes in consecutive games as Pittsburgh beat Baltimore, 43-23. Big Ben had victimized the Colts the previous week with over 500 yards in the air.

Birthdays: Ed Budde, 1940; Larry Little, 1945; Mark May, 1959; Roddy White, 1981; Danny Amendola, 1985; Jimmy Garoppolo, 1991; Jordan Howard, 1994

Trivia: Whose 122.5 quarterback rating in 2011, when he threw 45 TDs to just 6 INTs, ranks as the highest single-season mark in NFL history?

Trivia Answer: Aaron Rodgers

NOVEMBER

On This Date: On November 3, 1990, one of college football's most prolific passing duels took place as Houston defeated Texas Christian, 56-35. Houston's David Klinger threw for 563 yards and seven touchdowns. Meanwhile, TCU's Matt Vogler tossed five TDs to go along with 690 yards through the air.

Birthdays: Bronko Nagurski, 1908; Phil Simms, 1955; Darren Sharper, 1975; Damien Woody, 1977; Karlos Dansby, 1981; Tamba Hali, 1983; LaMarr Woodley, 1984; Colin Kaepernick, 1987

Trivia: What Houston Cougars quarterback left college in 2012 as the NCAA's all-time leader in total passing yards, touchdowns, and completions?

Trivia Answer: Case Keenum

NOVEMBER

On This Date: On November 4, 2007, the Patriots inched closer to a perfect regular season with a 24-20 defeat of the 7-0 Colts in one of the NFL's most-hyped regular season contests ever. The historic matchup came just hours after Adrian Peterson set a new single-game record with 296 yards rushing in a Vikings win over the Chargers.

Birthdays: Willie Buchanon, 1950; Steve Mariucci, 1955; Orlando Pace, 1975; Vince Wilfork, 1981; Devin Hester, 1982; Branden Albert, 1984; Brandon LaFell, 1986; Dez Bryant, 1988

Trivia: The Patriots finished off a perfect 2007 regular season by taking down what team, 38-35, in their finale?

Trivia Answer: New York Giants (The Giants, of course, would beat the Pats in the Super Bowl.)

NOVEMBER

On This Date: On November 5, 1995, the Carolina Panthers won an NFL expansion team record fourth game in a row as they defeated the San Francisco 49ers, 13-7. It was also the first time in league history that an expansion team defeated a defending Super Bowl champion.

Birthdays: Kellen Winslow, 1957; Todd Collins, 1971; Jason Kelce, 1987; Odell Beckham, Jr., 1992

Trivia: What Panther set a Super Bowl record for the longest offensive play from scrimmage, an 85-yard touchdown reception, in Super Bowl XXXVIII?

Trivia Answer: Muhsin Muhammad, in Carolina's loss to New England

NOVEMBER

On This Date: On November 6, 1869, Rutgers and Princeton met in New Brunswick, N.J., in the first college football game. Rutgers won, 6-4, in a contest that featured 25 players on each side and one-point "touchdowns". Because no throwing or running with the ball was permitted, the event more closely resembled a soccer match.

Birthdays: Pat Dye, 1939; Mark Haynes, 1958; Gerald Riggs, 1960; Erik Kramer, 1964; Derrick Alexander, 1971; Pat Tillman, 1976; Aaron Hernandez, 1989

Trivia: Years after he scored the first touchdown in Seahawks Super Bowl history, who married women's professional soccer goalie Hope Solo in 2012?

Trivia Answer: Jerramy Stevens

NOVEMBER

On This Date: On November 7, 1965, Bart Starr was sacked 11 times against the Detroit Lions in a Packers loss. Exactly 45 years later, another Green Bay legend, Brett Favre, threw for a career-high 446 yards. Favre, however, did it as a Viking. His team defeated Arizona in overtime.

Birthdays: Ray Renfro, 1929; Tommy Hart, 1944; Anthony Thomas, 1977; LeCharles Bentley, 1979

Trivia: The Bart Starr Award has been given annually to an NFL player since 1989. What is it for?

Trivia Answer: In honor of Starr serving as a positive role model, it's given to the player who best exemplifies outstanding character on the field and in the community.

NOVEMBER

On This Date: On November 8, 1970, Tom Dempsey kicked a record-breaking 63-yard field goal to give the Saints a 19-17 win over the Lions. Dempsey was born without toes on his right foot – his kicking foot. Matt Prater would top Dempsey's mark by hitting a 64-yard field goal in 2013.

Birthdays: Bobby Bowden, 1929; Jimmie Giles, 1954; Eric Martin, 1961; Qadry Ismail, 1970; Sam Bradford, 1987; Jeremy Kerley, 1988

Trivia: Playing By The Rules: A field goal attempt is blocked and bounces back to the kicker. May the kicker drop-kick it through the uprights?

Trivia Answer: Yes

NOVEMBER

On This Date: On November 9, 2011, Joe Paterno was fired by the Penn State board of trustees. While Paterno said he would retire as the head football coach after the season, his time was cut short amidst growing uproar over the handling of sexual abuse allegations against assistant coach Jerry Sandusky.

Birthdays: Roy Jefferson, 1943; Mark Fields, 1972; Owen Daniels, 1982; Kyle Rudolph, 1989

Trivia: In 1969, Joe Paterno turned down an NFL head coaching job that would be taken by a future Hall of Famer. What was the team?

Trivia Answer: Pittsburgh Steelers (Chuck Noll took the position.)

NOVEMBER

On This Date: On November 10, 1928, fabled football coach Knute Rockne gave his famous "Win one for the Gipper" halftime speech. George Gipp was a Notre Dame All-American who died of pneumonia in 1920. Rockne's underdog Fighting Irish went on to defeat Army, 12-6, at Yankee Stadium.

Birthdays: George Sauer, 1943; Les Miles, 1953; Mike McCarthy, 1963; Isaac Bruce, 1972; Donte' Stallworth, 1980; Zach Ertz, 1990; Teddy Bridgewater, 1992

Trivia: The Seahawks drafted Notre Dame's Rick Mirer #2 overall in 1993, eight picks before Mirer's college backfield mate. Who was this future NFL star?

Trivia Answer: Jerome Bettis

NOVEMBER

On This Date: On November 11, 1990, Derrick Thomas set an NFL single-game record with seven sacks against the Seattle Seahawks. Thomas almost had an eighth, but Seahawks quarterback Dave Krieg broke free of his grasp to throw a 25-yard TD pass in the closing seconds and give Seattle a stunning 17-16 victory.

Birthdays: Bobby Dodd, 1908; LaMont Jordan, 1978; Willie Parker, 1980; Victor Cruz, 1986; Mark Sanchez, 1986

Trivia: Selected fourth by the Chiefs, Derrick Thomas was one of four Hall of Famers taken within the first five picks of the 1989 NFL Draft. Can you name the other three?

Trivia Answer: Troy Aikman (drafted #1), Barry Sanders (#3) and Deion Sanders (#5)

NOVEMBER

On This Date: On November 12, 1995, Dan Marino surpassed Fran Tarkenton as the NFL's all-time leader in passing yardage. Marino's 333 yards passing on the day were not enough to overtake the Patriots, however, as they defeated the Dolphins, 34-17. Marino would later become the first QB in NFL history to pass for more than 60,000 yards (61,361).

Birthdays: Tuffy Leemans, 1912; Jack Butler, 1927; Ken Houston, 1944; Al Michaels, 1944; Cliff Harris, 1948; Steve Bartkowski, 1952; Lance Briggs, 1980; Kendall Wright, 1989; Allen Hurns, 1991

Trivia: Two QBs have over 7,000 yards passing in the postseason, while everyone else behind them has fewer than 6,000. Who are they?

Trivia Answer: Tom Brady and Peyton Manning

NOVEMBER

On This Date: On November 13, 1999, Wisconsin running back Ron Dayne broke the NCAA rushing record held by Ricky Williams in a victory over Iowa. Dayne finished the game with 216 yards and would end up with 6,397 for his career (over 7,000 counting bowl games).

Birthdays: Vinny Testaverde, 1963; Steve Christie, 1967; Michael Bennett, 1985

Trivia: Before his Wisconsin days, J.J. Watt played a single season of college football at what school in 2007?

Trivia Answer: Central Michigan

NOVEMBER

On This Date: On November 14, 1970, tragedy struck Marshall University when 75 people, including nearly 40 football players and much of the team's coaching staff, were killed in a plane crash near the Tri-State Airport in West Virginia. The team was returning from that day's game, a loss to East Carolina.

Birthdays: Mike Livingston, 1945; Joe Fields, 1953; Fredd Young, 1961; Dana Stubblefield, 1970; Lawyer Milloy, 1973; Kyle Orton, 1982; T.Y. Hilton, 1989

Trivia: Two Vikings All-Pro players went to school at Marshall - one in the '80s and the other in the '90s. Who are they?

Trivia Answer: Carl Lee and Randy Moss, respectively

NOVEMBER

On This Date: On November 15, 1964, Chiefs quarterback Len Dawson fumbled an NFL record seven times in a 28-14 loss to the Chargers. Ironically, the Chiefs as a team fumbled just seven times in the entire 2002 season to set a then-record.

Birthdays: Al Dorow, 1929; Otis Armstrong, 1950; Leon Gray, 1951; Cory Redding, 1980; Lofa Tatupu, 1982; Tyler Boyd, 1994

Trivia: In his first six NFL seasons with the Cardinals, this Super Bowl MVP running back fumbled the ball 48 times. In his final six years with the Giants, he fumbled just three times. Who is he?

Trivia Answer: Ottis Anderson

NOVEMBER

On This Date: On November 16, 1957, college football's longest winning streak came to an end. A Dick Lynch touchdown late in the fourth quarter was the only score as Notre Dame upset Oklahoma, 7-0. Up to that point, the Sooners had won 47 straight games.

Birthdays: Harvey Martin, 1950; Osi Umenyiora, 1981; Marcus McNeill, 1983

Trivia: Two undefeated college football squads entered the 1988 National Championship Game. Notre Dame defeated what team, 34-21, to claim its last title to date?

Trivia Answer: West Virginia

NOVEMBER

On This Date: On November 17, 1968, NBC cut away from the Raiders-Jets football game with a little more than a minute to play to show the movie *Heidi*. The network's offices were deluged with phone calls from angry fans who missed seeing Oakland score two touchdowns in nine seconds to beat New York, 43-32. The contest became forever known as the Heidi Game.

Birthdays: Kyle Vanden Bosch, 1978; Reggie Wayne, 1978; Nathan Vasher, 1981; Eric Winston, 1983

Trivia: In what short-lived TV sitcom that aired in 1978 did Joe Namath star as Joe Casey, a washed up athlete-turned high school basketball coach?

Trivia Answer: The Waverly Wonders

NOVEMBER 18

On This Date: On November 18, 1985, Redskins quarterback Joe Theismann suffered a gruesome career-ending injury when he was hit by Giants linebacker Lawrence Taylor. Theismann suffered a compound fracture of his right leg in the middle of a *Monday Night Football* game at RFK Stadium. The infamous moment was later used in the opening for the 2009 film *The Blind Side*.

Birthdays: Jack Tatum, 1948; Tony Franklin, 1956; Warren Moon, 1956; Todd Bowles, 1963; Seth Joyner, 1964; Raghib "Rocket" Ismail, 1969

Trivia: After a solid rookie year with New England, what runner blew out his knee in a beach flag football game and never returned to the Pats?

Trivia Answer: Robert Edwards

NOVEMBER 19

On This Date: On November 19, 1978, a "Miracle at the Meadowlands" occurred when the Giants blew a game vs. the Eagles by calling a run rather than a simple kneel down to seal a victory. Herman Edwards took advantage of a botched exchange between Giants QB Joe Pisarcik and back Larry Csonka, running in the fumble for the winning score. The final was 19-17, Philadelphia.

Birthdays: Ahmad Rashad, 1949; Richard Todd, 1953; Mike Mularkey, 1961; Larry Johnson, 1979; DeAngelo Hall, 1983; Alex Mack, 1985

Trivia: The Giants and Eagles played in the 2008 postseason in the first-ever NFL game that finished with a final score of 23-11. Who won?

Trivia Answer: Eagles

NOVEMBER

On This Date: On November 20, 1982, "The Play" took place at California Memorial Stadium. With Stanford up 20-19 after a field goal with seconds remaining, the California Bears returned the kickoff all the way for a touchdown on a series of laterals. The biggest obstacle to the end zone for the Bears was the Stanford school band, which was out on the field for a premature victory celebration. Cal won, 25-20.

Birthdays: Jack Rudnay, 1947; Mark Gastineau, 1956; Dwight Stephenson, 1957; Dabo Swinney, 1969; Joey Galloway, 1971; Tra Thomas, 1974; Zack Martin, 1990

Trivia: In his first Pro Bowl in 2011, what Browns lineman, a former Cal Golden Bear, recorded his first career touchdown in the game's final minute by running a lateral in for a score?

Trivia Answer: Alex Mack

NOVEMBER

On This Date: On November 21, 1982, the NFL resumed play after seven weeks of the season were lost due to the NFL Players Association strike. The Redskins would win the Super Bowl following a regular season that consisted of just nine games.

Birthdays: Sid Luckman, 1916; Jim Ringo, 1931; Troy Aikman, 1966; Michael Strahan, 1971; Danny Kanell, 1973; Justin Tucker, 1989

Trivia: What Redskin became the first-ever special teamer to win the MVP award after the 1982 strike-shortened season?

Trivia Answer: Mark Moseley

NOVEMBER

On This Date: On November 22, 2014, Samaje Perine of Oklahoma set an FBS record by rushing for 427 yards in a 44-7 Sooners win over Kansas. Perine broke the mark of 408 set by Wisconsin's Melvin Gordon just one week earlier.

Birthdays: Charley Johnson, 1938; Jack Reynolds, 1947; Mark Malone, 1958; Eric Allen, 1965; Derrick Johnson, 1982; Brian Hartline, 1986; Brock Osweiler, 1990; Giovani Bernard, 1991

Trivia: In 2004, Oklahoma's Adrian Peterson became the first freshman to finish second in the Heisman balloting. Who finished first?

Trivia Answer: USC's Matt Leinart

NOVEMBER

On This Date: On November 23, 1984, Doug Flutie's "Hail Mary" pass with six seconds left in the game fell into the hands of receiver Gerard Phelan to give Boston College a dramatic 47-45 win over Miami. Flutie and Miami QB Bernie Kosar combined for 919 passing yards on the day.

Birthdays: Daniel Snyder, 1964; Jamie Sharper, 1974; Mike Tolbert, 1985; Spencer Ware, 1991

Trivia: In 1991, #2 Miami took down what rival and #1-ranked team when Gerry Thomas missed a 34-yard field goal attempt with seconds remaining?

Trivia Answer: Florida State

NOVEMBER

On This Date: On November 24, 2011, John Harbaugh's Ravens took down Jim Harbaugh's 49ers, 16-6, in the first NFL game featuring brothers as opposing head coaches. The two would meet again, of course, in Super Bowl XLVII, where John's Ravens were again victorious.

Birthdays: John Henry Johnson, 1929; Yale Lary, 1930; Stan Jones, 1931; Jerry Mays, 1939; Paul Tagliabue, 1940; Ryan Fitzpatrick, 1982; Jimmy Graham, 1986

Trivia: What former NFL receiver's brother once served as the head coach of the NBA's Raptors?

Trivia Answer: Cris Carter (brother Butch Carter)

NOVEMBER

On This Date: On November 25, 1993, the Cowboys were on their way to a snowy Thanksgiving Day win...until Leon Lett came flying in. Up 14-13, Dallas blocked a Miami field goal attempt with seconds left. Inexplicably, Lett tried to recover the ball and slipped on the ice. Miami regained possession and won with a field goal at the gun.

Birthdays: Lenny Moore, 1933; Joe Gibbs, 1940; Chip Kelly, 1963; Bernie Kosar, 1963; Cris Carter, 1965; Donovan McNabb, 1976; Dan Carpenter, 1985

Trivia: In 1994, what Cowboys backup came up big on Turkey Day with over 300 yards and two touchdowns in a shootout win over the Packers?

Trivia Answer: Jason Garrett

NOVEMBER

On This Date: On November 26, 1989, the Rams scored 14 points in the final minutes of regulation before beating the Saints, 20-17, in overtime. Flipper Anderson scored the game-tying touchdown and set an NFL record with 336 receiving yards on 15 catches.

Birthdays: Jan Stenerud, 1942; Art Shell, 1946; Roger Wehrli, 1947; Harry Carson, 1953; Mike Merriweather, 1960; Jeff Jaeger, 1964

Trivia: What 2003 second round pick burst onto the scene when he set an NFL record for the most receiving yards by a rookie in his first game, with 217?

Trivia Answer: Anquan Boldin, with the Cardinals

NOVEMBER

On This Date: On November 27, 1966, the defense rested. The Redskins outscored the Giants, 72-41, in a game that set the NFL record for total points. In all, 16 touchdowns were scored. Washington kicked the lone field goal with seconds left to break the single-team mark of 70 points set by the Rams in 1950.

Birthdays: Ken O'Brien, 1960; Larry Allen, 1971; Jon Runyan, 1973; Martin Gramatica, 1975; Adam Archuleta, 1977; Michael Floyd, 1989

Trivia: A 51-45 Wild Card shootout in 2010 that ended in overtime set an NFL postseason record for total points. What two teams took part in it?

Trivia Answer: Cardinals and Packers

NOVEMBER

On This Date: On November 28, 1929, Chicago Cardinals running back Ernie Nevers set a record that may never be broken. He scored all 40 of his team's points in a blowout win over the Bears. Not only did Nevers account for six touchdowns...he kicked four extra points.

Birthdays: Ernie Ladd, 1938; Paul Warfield, 1942; Dave Duerson, 1960; Dale Carter, 1969; Freddie Mitchell, 1978; Jarvis Landry, 1992

Trivia: What rookie/veteran duo caught a combined 29 of their team's 41 passing touchdowns in their 15-1 season in 1998?

Trivia Answer: Randy Moss (17 TDs) and Cris Carter (12), of the Vikings

---

NOVEMBER

On This Date: On November 29, 1890, the very first Army-Navy football game was played at West Point, New York. The Midshipmen won, 24-0. Exactly 44 years later, the Detroit Lions began their annual NFL tradition when they played their first Thanksgiving home game, losing to the Chicago Bears, 19-16.

Birthdays: Damon Harrison, 1988; Russell Wilson, 1988; Sheldon Richardson, 1990; Stefon Diggs, 1993

Trivia: In 1989, the Eagles destroyed the Cowboys, 27-0, on Thanksgiving. The hotly-contested affair, in which Dallas coach Jimmy Johnson accused Philly coach Buddy Ryan of trying to hurt certain players, was given what nickname?

Trivia Answer: The Bounty Bowl

NOVEMBER

On This Date: On November 30, 1987, Bo Jackson put on a show for the *Monday Night Football* audience. He rushed for 221 yards and scored three TDs in his fifth NFL game as his Raiders beat Seattle, 37-14. Most memorable was his 91-yard score, untouched, down the sideline, and into the players' tunnel.

Birthdays: Cotton Davidson, 1931; Bill Walsh, 1931; Bo Jackson, 1962; Marcellus Wiley, 1974; Aaron Kampman, 1979

Trivia: On *Monday Night Football* in 1983, the longest run from scrimmage in NFL history took place when what back ran 99 yards for a score?

Trivia Answer: Tony Dorsett

DECEMBER

On This Date: On December 1, 2002, Michael Vick set a new single-game record for rushing yards by a quarterback with 173. The total included a 46-yard game-winning TD run in overtime as the Falcons topped the Vikings, 30-24. (Colin Kaepernick would later top Vick's mark.)

Birthdays: Steve Walsh, 1966; Todd Steussie, 1970; Jabar Gaffney, 1980; DeSean Jackson, 1986

Trivia: Set in 2013, who holds the NFL record for the longest touchdown run by a quarterback, at 93 yards?

Trivia Answer: Terrelle Pryor

DECEMBER

On This Date: On December 2, 1975, Ohio State running back Archie Griffin was named the Heisman Trophy winner – for the second straight year. Griffin, the first player to start in four Rose Bowls, would become a first round pick of the Bengals in 1976. He remains the only man to win the Heisman twice.

Birthdays: Willie Brown, 1940; O.J. McDuffie, 1969; Aaron Rodgers, 1983

Trivia: What 28-year-old quarterback was the winner of the 2000 Heisman Trophy?

Trivia Answer: Chris Weinke of Florida State

DECEMBER

On This Date: On December 3, 2000, NFL history was made when four players each had 200-yard rushing games. Mike Anderson, Corey Dillon, Warrick Dunn and Curtis Martin all surpassed the mark, led by Anderson's 251.

Birthdays: Tom Fears, 1922; Bobby Boyd, 1937; Cornelius Griffin, 1976; James Laurinaitis, 1986

Trivia: With 1,697, Curtis Martin topped what player by a single yard to win the 2004 NFL rushing title?

Trivia Answer: Shaun Alexander

DECEMBER

On This Date: On December 4, 1977, the Tampa Bay Buccaneers walked the plank to their 26th consecutive loss, 10-0, to the Bears. After being shut out in four of their last five games, the expansion franchise's first win ever would come the following week against New Orleans – a 33-14 triumph.

Birthdays: Frank Reich, 1961; Jeff Blake, 1970; Joe Thomas, 1984

Trivia: What team's heartbreaking last-second loss to the Steelers in the 2015 postseason marked their eighth consecutive playoff defeat?

Trivia Answer: Cincinnati Bengals

DECEMBER

On This Date: On December 5, 1976, Bills running back O.J. Simpson ran for 200 yards for the sixth and final time of his NFL career. Exactly 32 years later, the Juice was sentenced to a maximum of 33 years in prison on charges of kidnapping and armed robbery. Simpson had led a group that broke into a Las Vegas hotel room and attempted to steal sports memorabilia.

Birthdays: Jim Plunkett, 1947; Jim Tressel, 1952; Art Still, 1955; Art Monk, 1957; Charlie Batch, 1974; LeGarrette Blount, 1986; Kyle Long, 1988; Jurrell Casey, 1989

Trivia: The 2015 Buffalo Bills became the first team in NFL history with two 100-yard rushers and a 150-yard receiver in the same game. Who were they?

Trivia Answer: LeSean McCoy and Karlos Williams were the backs, and Sammy Watkins the receiver.

DECEMBER

On This Date: On December 6, 2009, Vikings quarterback Brett Favre broke Jim Marshall's NFL record among position players when he took part in his 283rd consecutive regular season game, a 30-17 loss to Arizona. Favre's iron man streak would end at 299 the following year.

Birthdays: Otto Graham, 1921; Andy Robustelli, 1925; Darrell Jackson, 1978; Robbie Gould, 1981; Johnny Manziel, 1992

Trivia: When Brett Favre first arrived in Green Bay, he briefly sat behind what Pro Bowl quarterback who would leave the Packers following the 1992 season?

Trivia Answer: Don Majkowski

DECEMBER

On This Date: On December 7, 1963, CBS unveiled a broadcast innovation during the Army-Navy game. The network used instant replay to showcase the many moves of the Midshipmen's scrambling quarterback, Roger Staubach. Staubach's team won, 21-15.

Birthdays: Rickey Young, 1953; Terrell Owens, 1973; Al Harris, 1974; Alan Faneca, 1976

Trivia: The father of what NFL coaching great served as an assistant coach at Navy for over three decades?

Trivia Answer: Bill Belichick (father Steve)

DECEMBER

On This Date: On December 8, 1940, Chicago crushed Washington, 73-0, in the NFL Championship Game. The Redskins had more passing yardage than the Bears and the same number of first downs, but Chicago pulled down eight interceptions. Just three weeks earlier, Washington had defeated Chicago, 7-3.

Birthdays: Bob Brown, 1941; Bill Polian, 1942; George Rogers, 1958; Jeff George, 1967; Barry Foster, 1968; Philip Rivers, 1981; Sam Shields, 1987

Trivia: What Bear made NFL history in 2001 with back-to-back overtime interception returns for scores to beat the 49ers and Browns in consecutive weeks?

Trivia Answer: Mike Brown

DECEMBER

On This Date: On December 9, 1934, the Giants defeated the Bears, 30-13, to win the NFL championship in the "Sneakers Game." The Giants scored 27 unanswered points in the second half after switching to basketball sneakers for better footing on the frozen Polo Grounds surface.

Birthdays: Deacon Jones, 1938; Dick Butkus, 1942; Jim Haslett, 1955; Al "Bubba" Baker, 1956; David Akers, 1974

Trivia: Following the death of Johnny Unitas in 2002, what Ravens quarterback and fellow Louisville alum wore a pair of Unitas' signature black high-top cleats in a game as a tribute?

Trivia Answer: Chris Redman

DECEMBER

On This Date: On December 10, 1989, Steve Largent became the first NFL player to catch 100 touchdown passes in a career. Exactly 17 years later, LaDainian Tomlinson scored his 29th TD of the year, topping the single-season mark which had been recently set by Shaun Alexander. L.T. would finish with 31.

Birthdays: Grady Alderman, 1938; D'Brickashaw Ferguson, 1983; Matt Forte, 1985; Eric Reid, 1991

Trivia: Who is the only NFL player to score at least one touchdown in 20 straight seasons?

Trivia Answer: Jerry Rice

DECEMBER

On This Date: On December 11, 1993, Florida State quarterback Charlie Ward was named the Heisman Trophy winner by one of the largest margins in the history of the voting. Ward would be selected by the New York Knicks in the first round of the 1994 NBA Draft.

Birthdays: Doc Blanchard, 1924; Del Shofner, 1934; Fred Cox, 1938; Errict Rhett, 1970; Willie McGinest, 1971; Vonnie Holliday, 1975; Roman Harper, 1982

Trivia: What two Pro Bowl players from Syracuse and North Carolina are the only men to ever play on both NCAA Final Four and Super Bowl teams?

Trivia Answer: Donovan McNabb (Eagles) and Julius Peppers (Panthers), respectively

DECEMBER

On This Date: On December 12, 1965, two of the NFL's legendary running backs combined for eleven touchdowns. Paul Hornung scored five TDs in a Packers win over the Colts, while rookie Gale Sayers was even more productive with six scores in a Bears triumph over the 49ers.

Birthdays: Ray Brown, 1962; Mike Golic, 1962; Haywood Jeffires, 1964; John Randle, 1967; Nate Clements, 1979; Ronnie Brown, 1981; Andrew Whitworth, 1981; Brad Smith, 1983; T.J. Ward, 1986; Alfred Morris, 1988; Mike Glennon, 1989; Tyron Smith, 1990

Trivia: In 2012, what runner was the last non-quarterback to be named the NFL's MVP?

Trivia Answer: Adrian Peterson

DECEMBER

On This Date: On December 13, 2009, Denver's Brandon Marshall set an NFL single-game record with 21 catches against the Colts. Marshall finished with 200 yards receiving and two touchdowns. Even so, the Broncos lost to Indy, 28-16.

Birthdays: Lemar Parrish, 1947; Richard Dent, 1960; Gary Zimmerman, 1961; Rex Ryan, 1962; Fletcher Cox, 1990

Trivia: In 2000, who became the first player in NFL history to catch 20 passes in a single game?

Trivia Answer: Terrell Owens

DECEMBER

On This Date: On December 14, 1991, less than a month after striking the Heisman pose when he scored on a punt return, Michigan's Desmond Howard was named the Heisman Trophy winner in a runaway vote.

Birthdays: Charley Trippi, 1921; Adrian Burk, 1927; Ernie Davis, 1939; Randy Starks, 1983

Trivia: Who became the first freshman to win the Heisman Trophy in 2012?

Trivia Answer: Texas A&M's Johnny Manziel

DECEMBER

On This Date: On December 15, 1968, Philadelphia fans infamously booed Santa Claus as the Eagles hosted the Vikings at Franklin Field. The person hired to play Santa in a halftime parade was nowhere to be found. After a last-minute replacement was pulled from the stands, fans gave him the business as he took the field.

Birthdays: Joe Walton, 1935; Nick Buoniconti, 1940; Jerry Ball, 1964; Rodney Harrison, 1972; Josh Norman, 1987

Trivia: What future Hall of Fame Cowboy suffered a career-ending injury in Philadelphia in 1999 and was mercilessly cheered by Eagles fans as he went off on a stretcher?

Trivia Answer: Michael Irvin

DECEMBER

On This Date: On December 16, 1973, O.J. Simpson became the first player in NFL history to rush for 2,000 yards in a single season. Simpson reached the mark with 200 yards on the ground in a Bills 34-14 win over the Jets in the season finale.

Birthdays: Buddy Parker, 1913; Bart Oates, 1958; Jerry Gray, 1962; William "Refrigerator" Perry, 1962; Antrel Rolle, 1982; David Johnson, 1991

Trivia: In 2004, who became the second of only two men (after Barry Sanders) to rush for 1,000 yards in each of his first 10 NFL seasons?

Trivia Answer: Curtis Martin

DECEMBER

On This Date: On December 17, 1933, the NFL held its first Championship Game, at Chicago's Wrigley Field. The Bears, led by Bronko Nagurski, edged the New York Giants, 23-21.

Birthdays: Russ Washington, 1946; Eddie Brown, 1962; Tony Richardson, 1971; Takeo Spikes, 1976

Trivia: In 2010, Wrigley Field was the site of a unique college football game between Illinois and Northwestern. Why were all offensive plays run towards one end of the field?

Trivia Answer: Because the east end zone was so close to the right field wall. (The Fighting Illini won, 48-27.)

DECEMBER

On This Date: On December 18, 1932, the first-ever NFL playoff game took place as the Chicago Bears defeated the Portsmouth Spartans, 9-0, for the title. After the two teams finished the year with identical records, the game was scheduled to determine the league champion.

Birthdays: Greg Landry, 1946; Don Beebe, 1964; Marco Coleman, 1969; Peter Boulware, 1974; Ben Watson, 1980; Pierre Thomas, 1984

Trivia: As the head coach of the Cleveland Browns, Bill Belichick won his first career playoff game against what team in 1994?

Trivia Answer: New England Patriots

DECEMBER

On This Date: On December 19, 2010, the Eagles shocked the Giants, 38-31, in the "Miracle at the New Meadowlands." After trailing by 21 with under eight minutes to play, Philly came back to tie it. DeSean Jackson then won the game on a walk-off punt return TD as time expired.

Birthdays: Bobby Layne, 1926; Reggie White, 1961; Randall McDaniel, 1964; Warren Sapp, 1972; Jake Plummer, 1974

Trivia: True or False? There has never been a punt return touchdown in the Super Bowl.

Trivia Answer: True

DECEMBER

On This Date: On December 20, 1980, NBC broadcast a game between the Jets and Dolphins without announcers. Viewers were aided by graphics and the stadium's public address system in this one-time experiment. Exactly 23 years later, an inebriated Joe Namath appeared alongside ESPN sideline reporter Suzy Kolber. Unfortunately for Broadway Joe, there was plenty of audio for this Jets-Patriots game.

Birthdays: Bob Hayes, 1942; Nate Newton, 1961; Rich Gannon, 1965; Roy Williams, 1981; LenDale White, 1984; Malcolm Jenkins, 1987; Martavis Bryant, 1991

Trivia: What former Broncos star retired from ESPN in 2016 after nearly 30 years with the network?

Trivia Answer: Tom Jackson

DECEMBER

On This Date: On December 21, 1997, Barry Sanders became the third player in NFL history to rush for 2,000 yards in a season. Exactly 11 years later, the Sanders-less Lions became the NFL's first 0-15 team after a 42-7 loss to the Saints. Detroit, of course, would finish the season 0-16.

Birthdays: Joe Paterno, 1926; Mike Alstott, 1973; Mark Ingram, 1989; Ha Ha Clinton-Dix, 1992

Trivia: Who coached the Lions during their infamous 0-16 season in 2008?

Trivia Answer: Rod Marinelli

DECEMBER

On This Date: On December 22, 1946, Otto Graham led his Cleveland Browns to a 14-9 victory over the New York Yankees at Cleveland Stadium in the first All-America Football Conference Championship Game. The Browns would win all four of the AAFC's titles before the league disbanded and they were admitted to the NFL for the 1950 season.

Birthdays: Ray Guy, 1949; Dennis Northcutt, 1977; Everson Griffen, 1987; Cecil Shorts, 1987

Trivia: Following his playing days, Otto Graham spent three unsuccessful seasons as the head coach of what NFL team?

Trivia Answer: Washington Redskins

DECEMBER

On This Date: On December 23, 1972, Franco Harris made the "Immaculate Reception" that advanced the Steelers to the AFC Championship Game. Trailing the Raiders, 7-6, with under 30 seconds to go, Terry Bradshaw threw a fourth-down desperation pass. The throw bounced off an Oakland defender and into the hands of Harris, who ran 42 yards for the winning score.

Birthdays: Paul Hornung, 1935; Willie Wood, 1936; Jack Ham, 1948; Jim Harbaugh, 1963; Alge Crumpler, 1977

Trivia: The longest touchdown pass of Terry Bradshaw's NFL career went for 90 yards. What fellow quarterback was on the receiving end?

Trivia Answer: Mark Malone (The catch would be the first, and last, of his career.)

DECEMBER

On This Date: On December 24, 1967, Joe Namath became the first quarterback in NFL history to throw for 4,000 yards in a single season, doing so in a 14-game season. He reached the mark with 343 yards passing in a win against the Chargers. Namath's feat would not be matched for another 12 years, when Dan Fouts joined him.

Birthdays: Bill Dudley, 1921; Michael Haynes, 1965; Tim Jennings, 1983; Davante Adams, 1992

Trivia: While no other player has done it more than once, what quarterback has thrown for over 5,000 yards in a season five times in his career?

Trivia Answer: Drew Brees

DECEMBER

On This Date: On December 25, 1971, Miami and Kansas City played the NFL's longest game. The outcome wasn't decided until the Dolphins' Garo Yepremian kicked a 37-yard field goal more than 22 minutes into sudden-death overtime. Miami advanced in the playoffs with the 27-24 win.

Birthdays: Dave Parks, 1941; Ken Stabler, 1945; Larry Csonka, 1946; William Andrews, 1955; Hanford Dixon, 1958; Marcus Trufant, 1980; Demaryius Thomas, 1987

Trivia: The Chiefs, in the 2003 Divisional round, were a part of the first playoff game in NFL history that did not have a punt by either team. Who was their opponent?

Trivia Answer: Indianapolis Colts, who won, 38-31

DECEMBER

On This Date: On December 26, 1960, Philadelphia's Chuck Bednarik stopped Jim Taylor near the 10-yard line as time expired in the NFL Championship Game, preserving a 17-13 win over the Packers. Exactly five years later, Buffalo defeated the Chargers for a second consecutive time in the AFL Championship Game. Neither the Eagles nor the Bills have won a title since.

Birthdays: Glenn Davis, 1924; Bill Yeoman, 1927; Tony Brackens, 1974; Chris Borland, 1990; Brandon Scherff, 1991; Trevor Siemian, 1991

Trivia: In a 1960 Eagles-Giants game, Chuck Bednarik blindsided what Giants great, giving him a severe concussion and causing him to miss an entire season?

Trivia Answer: Frank Gifford

DECEMBER

On This Date: On December 27, 1964, the Cleveland Browns defeated the Baltimore Colts, 27-0, in the NFL Championship Game. It would be the Browns' last title to date, and Cleveland's last major sports title until the NBA's Cavs won it all in 2016 over the Warriors.

Birthdays: Andre Tippett, 1959; Lorenzo Neal, 1970; James Stewart, 1971; Deuce McAllister, 1978; Carson Palmer, 1979; Bernard Berrian, 1980; Jamaal Charles, 1986

Trivia: Four teams have never played in a Super Bowl. Who are they?

Trivia Answer: Browns, Jaguars, Lions and Texans

DECEMBER

On This Date: On December 28, 1958, the NFL Championship was decided in sudden death for the first time. Alan Ameche's touchdown run after eight minutes of overtime gave the Colts a 23-17 win over the Giants at Yankee Stadium in what has been dubbed "The Greatest Game Ever Played."

Birthdays: Steve Van Buren, 1920; Elbie Nickel, 1922; James Brooks, 1958; Carlos Carson, 1958; Everson Walls, 1959; James Jett, 1970; Adam Vinatieri, 1972; Cedric Benson, 1982

Trivia: The Colts and Giants would again meet the following season for the 1959 NFL title. Which team came out on top?

Trivia Answer: Colts, 31-16

DECEMBER

On This Date: On December 29, 1978, Ohio State lost the Gator Bowl and their head coach. After a Clemson interception, Buckeyes coach Woody Hayes erupted and punched the Tiger player who picked off the ball. Hayes was relieved of his duties by the university. Four years later to the day, Alabama's Bear Bryant had a less tumultuous final game, as his Crimson Tide defeated Illinois in the Liberty Bowl.

Birthdays: Ray Nitschke, 1936; Wayne Huizenga, 1937; Sean Payton, 1963; Jay Fiedler, 1971; Laveranues Coles, 1977; Eric Berry, 1988; Travis Benjamin, 1989; Myles Garrett, 1995

Trivia: In 2010, Andre Johnson became the first NFL player with 60 catches in each of his first eight seasons. In the game he set the mark, he infamously got into a fight with what Titans cornerback?

Trivia Answer: Cortland Finnegan

DECEMBER

On This Date: On December 30, 1973, the Miami Dolphins defeated the Oakland Raiders, 27-10, to win their third consecutive AFC title. Miami thus became the first team in NFL history to make it to three consecutive Super Bowls. They would go on to beat the Vikings.

Birthdays: Jim Marshall, 1937; Mel Renfro, 1941; Jim Nance, 1942; Kerry Collins, 1972; Patrick Kerney, 1976; Dominic Raiola, 1978; Carson Wentz, 1992

Trivia: Who were the three teams that the Eagles lost to in the NFC Championship Game from 2001-2003?

Trivia Answer: St. Louis Rams (2001), Tampa Bay Buccaneers (2002) and Carolina Panthers (2003)

DECEMBER

On This Date: On December 31, 1967, Bart Starr's one-yard plunge with 13 seconds remaining gave the Packers a 21-17 win over the Dallas Cowboys in the "Ice Bowl" for their third straight NFL title. Over 50,000 fans braved well-below-zero temperatures at Green Bay's Lambeau Field.

Birthdays: Hugh McElhenny, 1928; Don James, 1932; Heath Shuler, 1971; Jason Campbell, 1981

Trivia: In 2003, the Packers lost a playoff game for the first time ever at Lambeau. Who beat them 27-7?

Trivia Answer: Atlanta Falcons